"Through Eric's writing, God's truth catches me off guard. I think I'm enjoying a comical story about one of Eric's adventures when all of a sudden I get a piece of Wisdom lodged in my brain. Eric is observant and insightful. He notices things in Scripture and in life that many of us miss and then invites us to think through these observations as deeper levels."

— BRUXY CAVEY, teaching pastor at The Meeting House (www.themeetinghouse.ca) and author of *The End of Religion* (www.theendofreligion.org)

PLASTIC JESUS

Exposing the Hollowness of Comfortable Christianity

ERIC SANDRAS, PhD

NAVPRESS®

BRINGING TRUTH TO LIFE

OUR GUARANTEE TO YOU

We believe so strongly in the message of our books that we are making this quality guarantee to you. If for any reason you are disappointed with the content of this book, return the title page to us with your name and address and we will refund to you the list price of the book. To help us serve you better, please briefly describe why you were disappointed. Mail your refund request to: NavPress, P.O. Box 35002, Colorado Springs, CO 80935.

The Navigators is an international Christian organization. Our mission is to advance the gospel of Jesus and His kingdom into the nations through spiritual generations of laborers living and discipling among the lost. We see a vital movement of the gospel, fueled by prevailing prayer, flowing freely through relational networks and out into the nations where workers for the kingdom are next door to everywhere.

NavPress is the publishing ministry of The Navigators. The mission of NavPress is to reach, disciple, and equip people to know Christ and make Him known by publishing life-related materials that are biblically rooted and culturally relevant. Our vision is to stimulate spiritual transformation through every product we publish.

ISBN 1-57683-923-0

Cover design by Wes Youssi/www.thedesignworksgroup.com
Cover illustration photo by Steve Gardner, www.shootpw.com.
Creative Team: Terry Behimer, Liz Heaney, Darla Hightower, Collette Knittel, Arvid Wallen, Kathy Guist

Some of the anecdotal illustrations in this book are true to life and are included with the permission of the persons involved. All other illustrations are composites of real situations, and any resemblance to people living or dead is coincidental.

Unless otherwise identified, all Scripture quotations in this publication are taken from the HOLY BIBLE: NEW INTERNATIONAL VERSION® (NIV®). Copyright © 1973, 1978, 1984 by International Bible Society. Used by permission of Zondervan Publishing House. All rights reserved. The other version used is: *THE MESSAGE* (MSG). Copyright © 1993, 1994, 1995, 1996, 2000, 2001, 2002. Used by permission of NavPress Publishing Group.

Published in association with the literary agency of Leslie H. Stobbe, 300 Doubleday Road, Tryon, NC 28782.

Sandras, Eric, 1965-
    Plastic Jesus : exposing the hollowness of comfortable Christianity
/ Eric Sandras.
        p. cm.
    Includes bibliographical references.
    ISBN 1-57683-923-0
    1. Christian life.   I. Title.
    BV4501.3.S275 2006
    243--dc22
2006010026

Printed in the United States of America

1 2 3 4 5 6 / 10 09 08 07 06

FOR A FREE CATALOG OF
NAVPRESS BOOKS & BIBLE STUDIES,
CALL 1-800-366-7788 (USA)
OR 1-800-839-4769 (CANADA)

Dedicated to my mother:

*Those who know her know a woman of
generosity, selflessness, and care.
I know her as even more.*

CONTENTS

ACKNOWLEDGMENTS

Though my fingers do the typing, many lives influence the words:

Dan Rich: Integrity and vision seem to guide you. Thanks for allowing me to be a part of NavPress.

Liz Heaney: Skill, encouragement, and speed. Indeed you are a woman on a mission from God.

My Vineyard Family: We may not be religious, but we are serious about God. You've shown me the soil of healthy community is the best place to grow.

First Nations Friends: My worldview is wider and my faith deeper because of you.

Those in 12-Steps and Recovery: In every day of surrender to God there is renewed freedom for you and further inspiration for me. Continue to live God's story.

Dakota Jasmine and Carter William: Being your father will always be more rewarding than fame or finances. Pursue Jesus' footsteps while you learn from mine.

Cynthia: Every year I think I could not love you more deeply, but sixteen years continue to prove me wrong.

CHAPTER ONE

WHEN SUBURBIA LOSES ITS APPEAL

"HOW ARE THE BREASTS?" His question brought me out of my stupor and focused my attention back to the task at hand. No doubt this dapper forty-something's silicone-invested wife purposely had her assets on display, but I was a waiter *and* a purported follower of Christ. Both roles had momentarily been put on the backburner in lieu of this visual burden.

"Whoa. I'm sorry for being so rude; please forgive me," I muttered, swallowing my pride and lifting my eyes to make contact with Mr. Dapper.

Oddly, his face was buried in the menu and not glaring at me.

"What do you mean? You're not being rude. I was just wondering which of the specials you recommend—the Chicken Breast Oscar or the Hazelnut Shrimp."

That was close. I breathed a sigh of relief.

"Go with the Hazelnut Shrimp," I suggested, partly because I wanted nothing more to do with breasts for a few minutes.

"And for you ma'am, what can I get for you?" I asked, returning to Mrs. Silicone, this time with disciplined eyes.

"I've lost my appetite. Just give me a salad."

I detected a bit of cayenne bite in her response. A bite not directed at me, but to Mr. Dapper across the table.

I'd been a waiter long enough to know when a couple has brought into public something that should have been dealt with in the car, and I knew trouble was brewing.

"Right away," I responded, making a hasty retreat.

Sure enough, as the evening unfolded, Ken and Barbie unraveled. She left with tears; he left without remembering my tip. Oh, well. On this night I'd rather be broke than broken.

Who would've guessed it? Of all the people I run into during my everyday, hurry-up-and-wait life, who would have thought that this suburban couple, who shined with success and good looks on the outside, could have been experiencing so much decay underneath? They had likely driven to the restaurant in a nice car and flashed their freshly whitened teeth while palming the maître d' a twenty in order to get a preferred seat in the restaurant (due to the water view, not the waiter view). All so that they could enjoy a pleasant make-believe evening. But something was percolating underneath that exterior of perfection. Something painful, something avoided, and something that needed to get out.

Not What We Appear to Be

The suburbs are filled with picture-perfect couples who live in picture-perfect houses that could double as palaces in most third-world countries. One could naïvely drive through these communities, see the manicured lawns and oil-free driveways, and assume that, since all is well outside, all must be well on the inside.

But we are not that naïve. We know money can't buy happiness. It can only buy the therapy that helps us cope without it.

We know that a big house can't buy close family relationships. It can only create more room for family members to hide from each other. We know that a powerful SUV doesn't provide freedom. It only provides the illusion that, "If I really wanted to, I could leave the pavement that surrounds my life."

No, life in suburbia is not always what it appears to be. Author David Brooks agrees.

He writes these insightful words:

> America, especially suburban America, is depicted as a comfortable but somewhat vacuous realm of unreality: consumerist, wasteful, complacent, materialistic, and self-absorbed. Sprawling, shopping, Disneyfied Americans have cut themselves off from the sources of enchantment, the things that really matter. They have become too concerned with small and vulgar pleasures, pointless one-upmanship, and easy values. They have become at once too permissive and too narrow, too self-indulgent and too timid. Their lives are distracted by a buzz of trivial images, by relentless hurry instead of genuine contemplation, information rather than wisdom, and a profusion of superficial choices.[1]

Well said, Brooks. But while Brooks is pointing fingers at literal suburbia, Jesus is pointing his finger at a different location—spiritual suburbia. Only the true light of God can help us put into words what we have been sensing for quite some time—that all is not well in spiritual suburbia.

My Own Epiphany

Many years ago, I moved out of literal suburbia and drifted into the rural community of Port Angeles, Washington. It's a small timber town on the outer edges of the state. Surrounded by enormous rainforests, mountains, and the Pacific Ocean, Port Angeles invites its inhabitants to live any way but complacently. Ironically, as I left physical suburbia, my heart moved right into spiritual suburbia.

I may have been in a different neighborhood, but my life filled up with busyness just like before. My external world was spinning faster than a merry-go-round on Ecstasy. I was simultaneously starting a new church with seven friends, learning to parent a three-year-old and a newborn, teaching Human Sexuality at a local college, and trying to finish my doctoral dissertation. The harder I worked to keep the exterior stuff moving forward, the more I felt my faith and relationship with Christ begin to drift backward.

Now don't get me wrong. I was doing *good* things. But it took me a few years to realize that sometimes *good* things can be the greatest enemy to the intimate things that need to happen in our core.

Then one day as I stood and looked at my life, I knew, theologically, that the kingdom of God—the rule and reign of God—covered an expanse beyond all I could imagine in the external world. All that I could see, hear, and breathe was under the sovereign hand of God, and as a follower of Christ, I had been invited to live within such a reality. When Jesus said, "Repent, for the kingdom of heaven is near" (Jesus@ Matthew4:17), he literally was saying, "Think again about how you live your life, for God's rule and reign and power and forgiveness changes everything."

Wow, that looks good on paper, but how do I live out that reality?

And that was my problem. Sure, my spiritual life looked good on the outside. I was doing the "right" things—going on mission trips, planting churches, attending church—I even placed an extra few percent in the offering here and there. But the kingdom of God was not advancing inside my heart. In the distance, I could hear a calling, a beckoning of sorts, to come and explore the deeper realities of the kingdom of God.

Oddly, as I took time to listen, the beckoning came from some untouched and unexplored areas within my being, from the fenced off and uncharted parts of my soul. God was inviting me to explore the richness and meaning of his life-giving presence within me. I was at a crossroads. Was I willing to follow him into some unexplored territory?

The kingdom of God within? I already know a lot about prayer, study, and ritual. Jesus loves me this I know, for the Bible tells me so. What else is there?

The Holy Spirit replied, "I'm not hollow, but your faith *is* shallow. Now let my kingdom come, my will be done in you as it is in heaven."

Wow. There is a big difference between intellectual theology and practical theology. I had been living in a spiritual suburbia with nice sidewalks and picket fences around my Christianity. In the back of my mind, I knew that God was inviting me to explore some uncharted territories with him. I had allowed myself to be duped into thinking that the perceived safety of the predictable was more rewarding than the risk and joy of discovery. This drift had caused my faith to appear all put together on the outside. You know—do the right things . . . know the right people . . . speak the right "Christianese" . . . Yet as my faith became more neat and tidy on the outside, on the inside it grew more and more superficial.

Suburbia is full of icons. Big SUVs, large cookie-cutter houses, televisions, toys, and chrome toasters. Faith has its icons as well. Shiny crosses around our necks, Scripture verses plastered across our T-shirts, and fishes gracing our bumpers. Icons aren't bad if they lead us to something more real. But when they become a surrogate for reality, they leave us with something far less than what we truly need.

"Got Jesus?"

"Yep, I got a plastic bobblehead Jesus nodding on my dashboard. Pretty cool, huh?"

"Is that enough Jesus to carry you through life?"

"Probably not. That's why I got a marble Buddha on my coffee table."

Comfortable Christianity, with all its icons, can lull us into a state of ignorant bliss. Everything seems neat and tidy—plastic, so to speak. But if we stop and feel deep down in our souls, we're missing something. We've substituted a hollow structure for the real life that Jesus offers. If you are beginning to stare at your plastic Jesus and hear no answer, it is time to choose. Either follow that longing for substance a little further, or admire your little plastic buddy a bit more and pretend everything is fine.

Jeremiah tells of similar travelers who have come to a crossroads. "Stand at the crossroads and look; ask for the ancient paths, ask where the good way is, and walk in it, and you will find rest for your souls" (Jeremiah@6:16). It is clear that the travelers have never been here before, and they know they must choose a path. One path leads to impending doom; the other leads to a place where they will find peace for their souls.

What should these travelers do? How should they decide? They could rely on their own wisdom and knowledge of travel. But clearly the roads they have traveled don't guarantee success in the present. They could toss a coin, call a psychic, or even wish upon a star. But Jeremiah says there is a better way: Stand, look, ask, and listen. And that's exactly what we are going to do as we journey through this book together.

An Invitation to Look Inward

Are you in a similar place? Can you identify with this traveler and with me? Is there some God-given, yet uncharted, territory you need to explore? Are there places where you haven't gone spiritually, that have seemed too risky or insurmountable? Indeed, there is a vast expanse of terrain inside you that has yet to be conquered. But to get there, you must be willing to back out of the driveway and not travel the normal road of routine and ritual. You must be willing to stand, look, ask, and listen.

We've been lured into thinking that life in the suburbs of Christianity is as good as it gets. After all, we work hard to keep our lawns trimmed and tidy, our cars waxed and maintained, and our schedules juggled so that we can make it to the next event that our PDAs have reminded us we are late for.

We expend a lot of energy keeping our Christian doctrines all clean and form fitting, our appearances buffed up, and our lives organized around Christian meetings and conferences. But honestly, you call that adventure? At best, such a lifestyle is maintenance. At worst, it is counterfeit Christianity.

So perhaps now is a good time to stand. Stand and look at your life, and ask if you are living a life worth dying for. Is your faith shallow and your God hollow?

This book is an invitation to look inward. The presence of God not only invades our physical surroundings, but it can also invade our souls. Over the course of these pages I hope to share with you some of the icons of suburbia that have challenged and sometimes derailed my spiritual life. My goal is to lead you to a crossroads where you must decide whether you will explore the new territory in front of you or settle for the familiar you've grown to resent.

Will you follow an ancient path and find peace for your soul—or will you put up a protective fence around what you already know?

CHAPTER TWO

KEEPING UP WITH
THE JONESES

On Identity

THE OTHER DAY I was reading a blogsite in which the writer, who had heard me speak at a conference, referred to me as the "quintessential poster child for the metrosexual pastor." Okay. That short phrase contains a whole lot of verbiage, most of which I had to look up to understand.

I don't particularly like having sex on subways or trains, so why would someone say that I'm a metrosexual? And aren't poster children usually disabled or on the picture to solicit sympathy?

I jumped over to Google and did a search on *metrosexual.* Of course, any search containing the word *sex* is bound to yield some dangerous links. Nonetheless, curiosity got the better of me, even though I was sitting next to a couple of middle-aged church ladies at my local coffee shop, The Bella Rosa.

Wordspy.com yielded my answer:

metrosexual (met.roh.SEK.shoo.ul) n. An urban male with a strong aesthetic sense who spends a great deal of time and money on his appearance and lifestyle . . . A metrosexual is a clotheshorse wrapped around a dandy fused with a narcissist. Like soccer star David Beckham, who has been known to paint his fingernails, the metro-sexual is not afraid to embrace his feminine side. Why "metrosexual"? The metro- (city) prefix indicates this man's purely urban lifestyle, while the -sexual suffix comes from "homosexual," meaning that this man, although he is usually straight, embodies the heightened aesthetic sense often associated with certain types of gay men.[1]

Hey, I resemble those remarks. . . .

I mean it's not like I'm a candidate for the cable television hit *Queer Eye for the Straight Guy*, the show where five highly fashionable gay men attack and transform some unaware, underdressed, undereducated, and undersocialized jock whose hip, Barbie-doll girlfriend signed him up for a makeover.

Actually, just the other day I was looking in my closet and noticed a wide array of Hawaiian shirts. What great inventions those things are for guys. They match any color pants or shorts we wear. Plus, they hide any stain that we put on them—whether mustard, wine, or Brie. And where else can you find a shirt that is so floral and yet so irresistibly masculine? Last season, when they were in fashion, I definitely felt like the Big Kahuna.

Yep, I could walk around most any church conference in the middle of winter, and it was like springtime on the islands. Everyone cool had on a Hawaiian shirt and sported a tightly cropped goatee. All we needed was Don Ho leading worship, and the set would have been complete.

But this year is a different story. As I've walked around the malls and attended emergent church conferences, I've felt a little out of place. Hawaii is not hip this year. No, this year it is the retro T-shirt and trucker hats for the guys, and pink and black for the ladies. I'm thankful mullets aren't back in style yet because I am still shaving my head and holding on to my soul-patch goatee to be edgy.

So I'm staring at my closet, wondering what to do with all my Hawaiian shirts. Suddenly they are not so avant-garde look-ing. They aren't even made in Hawaii.

How can I wear something not authentic when I'm trying to speak on authenticity?

Of course, the Philippines are islands too, but that is beside the point. No, what I really want is a cool retro T-shirt . . . maybe a "sugar daddy" one, or one that says, "I get pumped at Gold's Gym."

Yeah, that would be cool. I want to be cool. Being cool is part of ministering the gospel. The gospel is cool. Where's my credit card?

Okay, so maybe I am a bit of a metrosexual. But I don't find my identity in what I wear or in what others say about me. Okay, so I don't find *all* of my identity in what I wear or what others say about me. Man, I wish I hadn't read that blogsite. . . .

The whole Hawaiian-shirt-in-the-closet dilemma got me thinking about all the stuff we grab onto in our struggle to find our identity. This struggle is core to how we interact in this world.

What Kind of Soap Do You Use?

Think about it. What's the first question we typically ask people after we find out what their name is? We ask, "What do you do?"

- "Oh, I'm an audiovisual consultant for the school district." (Meaning, I set up projectors and deliver movies to the classroom.)

- "I'm a level-three domestic engineer." (Meaning, I'm a stay-at-home mom with three kids.)
- "I'm a visual-clarification specialist." (Meaning, I wash windows for a living.)
- "I play in a local rock 'n' roll band." (Meaning, I deliver pizzas.)

Why do we immediately ask people what they do for a living? Most of us ask because the answer helps us size a person up. It enables us to make all kinds of assumptions about a person's value and potential as a human being. This is pretty silly, if we stop to think about it. In God's eyes, our value has never been determined by our jobs. To God, this sort of question is about as relevant as asking people what kind of soap they use, or if they have a light above their stove.

I remember my first week as a university professor in the Northwest. We had a faculty get-together one evening to introduce new faculty members to old. A snooty little affair it was. On one side of the room sat a dessert buffet table, complete with an assortment of cheesecakes, tarts, and small little chocolate things that resembled rabbit droppings (I was told they were chocolate-covered blueberries). Next to the dessert table was a nice selection of wines and some fresh-brewed teas and coffees.

As I walked into the gathering in my best metrosexual attire, I realized I was clearly underdressed. *Oh well, I'm the new guy. I can get by with looking hip instead of stodgy*, I thought.

I felt a sharp tap on my shoulder, and as I spun around to see who it was, an empty coffee cup was shoved in my face. "Get me some more coffee with one sugar and no cream, young man," demanded a distinguished looking gray-haired man in a bow tie. He obviously thought I was one of the volunteer student waiters.

"Sure. No problem," I said. And honestly, it was no problem. I see myself as a servant above and beyond anything else. That's my calling, whether from the pulpit, the lectern, or the sidewalks of life. So I went and got the man's coffee.

When I returned, the distinguished gray hair was talking to the head of the psychology department. As I handed the gray hair his coffee with one sugar and no cream, the psychology chair introduced me, "Dr. Gray Hair, have you met Dr. Sandras, our new Human Sexuality professor?"

Dr. Gray Hair turned a nice shade of pink and muttered something about it being an honor to meet me and thanked me for helping him out with the coffee. He didn't mean to be rude earlier, he explained, it was just that he'd been busy at that moment.

Dude, you were alone, doing nothing, when you whacked me on the shoulder, I thought.

"No problem," I said with a smile.

How amazing it was that my status, my value as a human being, jumped so much higher when Dr. Gray Hair discovered I was a distinguished professor and not just some peon student. What a shame.

Yet those of us who live in spiritual suburbia do the same thing. We tend to base our identity and value on the same fickle and shallow things that our culture does. We are tempted to believe that we are what we do, what we have, and what others say about us. I know because I've struggled with each of these messages. I bet you have too.

▸STOP, ▸LOOK, & LISTEN

1. Make a list of words that define who you are. See if you can figure out whether you used more adjectives, verbs, or nouns. (If you need help, call your old English teacher; she probably misses you.) What does this tell you about yourself?

2. Now make a list of words other people use when they attempt to define you. Are there words in common between the lists? Are those words you are okay to live by? If not, what can you do to change?

You Are What You Do

Most of us are constantly bombarded with pressure to find our value in what we do. Most of us have grown up in a performance-oriented world and bow to its pressure without even realizing we are doing so.

It starts around the age of six. Around the same time mom dressed us up and took our picture in front of the house. She had a teary-eyed smile, like something wonderful and yet traumatic was about to happen, and she needed to take our picture just in case she never saw us again. Then, just as a huge yellow monster pulled up in front of our house, she hurried us out the door. Hundreds of screaming kids tried to escape as its mouth opened, but the troll behind the wheel kept them in place. Mom shoved us onto the school bus, and it whisked us away to the next twelve years of our lives.

At school, we not only learned about Dick and Jane, multiplication tables, and the fact that bigger kids have all the power, but we also learned about the power of a report card to shape a life. The message we picked up on when we brought home our first report card was that it was a subtle, yet merciless, force.

Soon, this message becomes all too clear: Kids with good grades are greeted and rewarded with hugs, kisses, and phrases like, "I'm so proud of you. What great grades. I love you so much." Kids with Titanic grades (below "C" level) are greeted with disapproval, disappointment, and an absence of hugs and kisses. We can't imagine a parent saying, "You got a D. That's not a very good grade. Come here so I can hug and kiss you and tell you I love you." Yet we have no problem imagining a parent saying, "You got an A. That's wonderful! Come here so I can hug and kiss you and tell you I love you."

There it is—the performance orientation. It is a staple in the diet of suburbia. Early on, we are taught that our value is based on our performance. Perform well and our value rises; perform poorly and our value drops quicker than the stocks in the tech crash of the nineties.

This way of thinking has been around since the Garden of Eden, when Eve and Adam bit into the fruit of the Tree of the Knowledge of Good and Evil. Most people think the fruit was of the apple variety. But the handwritten note I scribbled in the margin of my Bible a long time ago says, "The fruit was DoToBe." We have been partaking of this fruit ever since.

- You have to please others to be loved.
- You have to dress like this to be accepted.
- You have to talk like this to be cool.
- You have to sleep with me to be cherished.
- You have to act like this to have status.
- You have to have good evaluations to have a voice in the company.
- You have to *do* this *to be* that. . . .

But God invites us to eat from the Tree of Life, the BeToDo tree. God wants us to just *be* his, because then we will naturally find ourselves doing what is right, what is good, what is honorable.

- Just be loved by God, and you will find yourself loving others.
- Just be God's child, and you'll find you no longer strive for acceptance but walk in it.
- Just be your God-given talents, and you will experience so much less struggle and self-criticism.
- Just *be*, and you will begin *to do* all you were created for.

Eugene Peterson puts it this way: "Make a careful exploration of who you are and the work you have been given, and then sink yourself into that. Don't be impressed with yourself. Don't compare yourself with others. Each of you must take responsibility for doing the creative best you can with your own life" (Galatians@6:4-5, MSG).

If we want to escape spiritual suburbia, we can't let our performance define our value. This is not only true in our occupations, it's also true in our "spiritual service."

I heard something a while back that helped set me free of the need to perform in the church. It set me free to *fail*. It set me free to take some risks, to stumble forward into God's goodness, and to not have to impress the holier-than-thou people around me. Here is the truth that set me free:

Anything in the kingdom of God that is worth doing—is worth doing poorly.

Read that sentence again. Chew on it a moment and then spit it out if you don't like it. Many of us are afraid to fail, so we never even try to succeed. We are afraid of rejection or imperfection or looking foolish, so we submit to the obedience of our church's public opinion rather than to God's divine one.

Doing poorly doesn't mean doing things apathetically or irreverently. It means doing them humanly. . . . Yes, we want to do our best with what we have been given. But our identity is not found in what we do or how well we do it. A career is just that, a career. A ministry is just a ministry. It does not define our purpose or value. Only the Tree of Life can do that.

The pressure to find our identities in what we do can be immense. So can the pressure to find our identities in what we have. Trust me, I'm a doctor. I must know what I'm talking about. . . .

You Are What You Have

I'm working on this chapter at Roots Coffee, a hip and artsy espresso joint designed with the metrosexual in mind, when this guy comes up to me and comments on my laptop's looks and style.

"Dude, that's a sweet-looking machine. What ya got under the hood?" he says in his finest metrosexual lingo.

"This Dell packs a whopping 80 gig hard drive, one gig of RAM, with a DVD-RW, wireless Internet, and a 1.7 Pentium M processor all wrapped up in this titanium-colored 3.5 pound package," I respond in a humbly proud way.

I'm feeling pretty good about myself right now. I own something cool and powerful. Well, at least in the techno-geek, metrosexual world.

But I can remember the day when just *having* a laptop was a blessing. I didn't care if it was the best or the fastest, just that it had a word processor and some way to plug into the wall so I could get e-mail access at 56k. How shallow can I get? In a month (and for sure by the time you read this book) this Pentium-powered beast won't be the top-of-the-line anymore. Will I still feel proud to fire it up in public places, or will I start to hide in the corner while I type, secretly wishing I had *another guy's* laptop?

I have friends who drive nice cars and love it when people look at them as they drive by. I have friends who have nice homes and love it when people compliment them on their interior décor. I have friends who have nice teeth and smile all the time so people can reflect on their pearly whites. I have pastor friends who find their identity in how big their church is. I have Carhartt jeans-and-baseball-cap-wearing friends who own chainsaws and love to hang out with other guys who wear Carhartt jeans and baseball caps and own chainsaws. They love to compare length and cutting power and to share stories of conquering trees (they are *not* metrosexuals by any stretch of the imagination).

We all love things; we are all consumers. When we live in spiritual suburbia, we let our things define us: We look to them to tell us who we are and what our value is. We gather up our things and hope they will fulfill our longing for meaning and significance.

I mean, really, have you ever noticed the various sizes and types of Bibles people carry to church? You know what I'm talking about: those Bibles with twelve colored pencils sticking out or a swanky Thomas Kinkade cover; those giant twelve-pound KJVs with artificially tattered pages. Many times the people toting these Bibles are trying to communicate a lot more to us than "I love Jesus" or "I love the Word." They are attempting to lay claim to a high-ranking position in the spiritual hierarchy of the congregation.

(Of course, I'm immune to such jockeying for position. I only carry three versions of the Bible on my Palm PDA. I humbly poke to the requested passages before the common Christian can even find the table of contents in his or her paper Bible. "Don't worry," I say. "I'll just read it in the *New International Version* and *The Message*, since I have them both here in my Palm PDA that I got at Office Depot. . . . It also comes with a Bible commentary, Spurgeon's devotionals, and other tools to help me grow in my understanding of the Word. Bless the Lord, brothers and sisters . . . now where were we?")

If you haven't noticed the Bibles, perhaps you've observed how people place money in the offering. Isn't it amazing how tightly a one-dollar or five-dollar bill can be compressed so no one notices, while a fifty- or hundred-dollar bill "naturally" lays open in an offering plate? Oh, I could go on . . . in your church it may be BMWs, laptops, and suits that define status. In mine it's more like Harleys, tattoos, and body piercings. The item doesn't really matter, as long as it serves to create a spiritual façade.

But, as Solomon warns us in Ecclesiastes, when we look to things to define us and to give our life meaning, we are chasing the wind (Solomon@Ecclesiastes2:11). We can never grab hold of what we long for; it will only continue to elude us.

When I think of our propensity to chase after things, I think of my pit bull, Koki. She loves to chase bubbles. My kids will blow bubbles out in the yard, and Koki will leap after them with a vengeance, clamping her dragon-like teeth onto the bubbles, only to find a funny taste in her mouth. For a moment, she looks quizzical, wondering what happened to the bubble she was so sure she had caught. But then another, *more beautiful,* bubble catches her eye, and off goes, chasing that one. Koki will repeat this process until she's eaten so much air, she toots her own bubbles out her backside.

The moral of the story is this: Don't be like my dog. Stop trying to find value and significance by owning all the right stuff. At first, owning stuff seems harmless and fun—besides everyone else seems to be doing it. But, if we play the game too long, we'll end up with a bad taste in our mouths and dissatisfaction in our guts because we'll never find our value in things we have.

When we live in spiritual suburbia, we also try to find our identity in what others say about us. This can be really dicey, as you likely know.

You Are What Others Say

Jonathan, my worship leader friend, has an amazing ability to write worship songs in a matter of minutes. At times he gets inspiration for a song and just starts writing the words on a piece of paper. Other times he puts down his pencil and picks up his guitar and composes a song before his coffee even gets cold.

The beauty of this is that the following Sunday, when he leads worship, Jonathan can introduce the new song and immediately know whether people connect with it or not. Being an author is a bummer in that sense. I spend months writing and rewriting a manuscript, and then once I feel it's powerful and full of wisdom, I submit it to my editor. That's when the pain begins. My editor will not only correct my grammar, but will actually help straighten out some of my twisted theology.

Back to the laptop I go, reworking my masterpiece till it's just right (again). Then my editor will send it back for me to tweak a few more times, and then finally it goes to print. I have to wait a few more months until it makes it to the bookshelf of some store in Paducah, Kentucky, right next to the plastic bobblehead Jesus display.

The hope is that while it sits on the shelf with its attractive title and cover, people will pick it up, read it within the year, and take the time to submit a review on Amazon.com. Or, if someone sent me a note that said they were just about to end their life by swallowing an enormous golf ball or by carrying their lava lamp with them into the bathtub, but then they happened to be in a bookstore in Paducah, Kentucky, and my book called out to them. Upon reading it, their lives were forever changed. They cried, they laughed, they put away the golf balls and turned off their lava lamps. That would be awesome to hear. Or at least they could post a comment that said, "That was a good book." What I don't want to read is stuff like, "Good book, well, at least till you open it."

When people tell us good things about ourselves, particularly things such as how we helped them or how God used us to change their lives around, we feel that our lives are worthwhile and that we have value. The reverse is also true. When people complain about us or criticize us, we tend to internalize those things and feel bad and unworthy.

Isn't it amazing how one negative comment can wipe out twenty positive ones? Some people are almost obsessive in their need to be liked by everyone around them. They can be at church or school or the office and receive one awkward glance from someone, and suddenly the doubting begins. *What's the matter? What did I do? Are they talking about me? Why don't they like me? Why do they like her better?*

We feel good about ourselves when others compliment us; we feel bad about ourselves when they criticize us. Life becomes an emotional roller coaster that we can't get off of. Indeed, that is the power of words. I know adults who are still trying to prove their worth to others because they grew up being told they would never amount to anything. I know married women who feel unattractive because they were told as children that no one would ever "want" them. I know fifty-year-old men who are still striving to prove they have significance because when they were kids their parents told them that they were "an accident."

Our identities are so easily tainted by the words of others, especially by the influential people in our lives. Parents, coaches, teachers, and significant others use their tongues to cut and hack away at our esteem like swords in the hands of drunken warriors in a *Braveheart* scenario gone bad.

Yet when we enter a relationship with Jesus, he invites us to live from a whole new reality, one not influenced by others' opinions. (This is so suburbic.) No, he invites us to live from a much more stable place, a place where the truthful words of our Creator can be the rock on which we build our lives.

People have opinions; God has truth.

People have attitudes; God has perspective.

People have brokenness; God has wholeness.

People have loud mouths; God has a gentle whisper.

Listen carefully. God may want to tell you something about yourself. (By the way, when you are done listening, why don't you send me an e-mail letting me know what you think of this book? I really want you to like it. . . .)

▸STOP, ▸LOOK, & LISTEN

1. You are what you do; you are what you have; you are what others say about you. . . . Which if these do you find your identity bending toward the most?

2. Pay attention today to how you "size up" other people. Are you reinforcing one of spiritual suburbia's three identity-shapers in someone else's life?

Move to the Rainforest

In the Pacific Northwest we have giant rainforests. Some trees stand over a hundred-feet tall, yet they don't tip over in a windstorm or when the ground becomes soft with moisture because they are deeply rooted. Not only do the roots provide nutrients and water when the surface becomes arid, but they also provide stability and strength as the treetops sway and bend in the wind.

What if we moved out of spiritual suburbia and moved into the spiritual rainforest? What if we no longer looked to suburbic identity-shapers to tell us who we are? What if we found our identity in something much more stable and deep than just keeping up with the Joneses? What if our decision-making was guided by a force much more powerful than a television infomercial? God invites us into a relationship with him that enables us to live this way. When our identities are rooted in the truth of God's Word and character, we are able to move away from the pressure of spiritual suburbia and into our true identity.

Have you ever had a life-changing experience? An encounter with something that changed the way you interacted with life, from that moment on? An event that forever changed the way you viewed the future and the past?

God intends for our encounter with him to do just that. Our relationship with him isn't supposed to just be an add-on to our lives to spruce it up a bit, like the fancy air fresheners that I hang in my car to cover the smell of last week's spilled latte. God doesn't want to just cover the smell of the sins in our life. He wants to tear up the fabric of our life and make it new, stain-resistant, and inviting enough for others to walk on.

What a cute and cuddly phrase "find your identity in God" is. But we need to live that truth out in the real world, where the message that we are what we have, what we do, and what others say about us is as tangible as the coffee I'm sipping. In order to escape this spiritual suburbia, we have to be willing to change the way we interact with God and the world in which we live.

Here are three realities that have helped me to root my identity in God rather than in the shallow identity-shapers of spiritual suburbia.

Root Yourself in God's Total Acceptance

Not long ago I was reading this great passage about the baptism of Jesus:

> At that time Jesus came from Nazareth in Galilee and was baptized by John in the Jordan. As Jesus was coming up out of the water, he saw heaven being torn open and the Spirit descending on him like a dove. And a voice came from heaven: "You are my Son, whom I love; with you I am well pleased." (Mark@1:9-11)

I intended to continue to power through the rest of the verses on my way to the finish line (my goal that morning had been to just get to the end of the reading, not necessarily to learn anything), but I sensed the Holy Spirit telling me to look left. I turned my head to the left and only saw the wall staring back at me.

"Look left in the text, Eric," I sensed the Holy Spirit say again, this time probably rolling his eyes.

As I looked to the left side of Mark's gospel, I responded, "There's not much there."

"Exactly," came Wisdom's reply.

Suddenly it hit me, like a pile of exegetical commentaries. When God said this about Jesus, Jesus, the man, hadn't done anything yet. He hadn't turned water into wine, hadn't raised the dead or fed five-thousand people. Jesus hadn't healed any lepers or died on the cross. Yet, even though Jesus hadn't done anything, the Father makes a huge deal over him. The heavens opened up, and God's voice boomed words that many of us spend our whole lives trying to earn: "You are my son, whom I love. With you I am well pleased."

The Father's total love and acceptance for Jesus wasn't based on performance. It was based on relationship. Jesus was loved because of *whose* he was, not because of what he did.

The same is true for any child of God. Our value is based on *whose* we are, yet some of us live our entire lives in spiritual suburbia, trying to earn our heavenly Father's affection and acceptance, yet never experiencing it because we are trying so hard to earn what has already been given to us. We are performing to become worthy of our Father's love and acceptance rather than resting in the love and acceptance he has already given to us—before we ever did even one thing for him.

When we are rooted in God's total acceptance—when we are feasting from the "BeToDo" tree—we are like toddlers who are secure in their relationship with their parents. Research shows that toddlers who have this sense of security are the most willing to explore and leave their parent's sight, looking for adventure, but that children with unpredictable or neglectful parents tend to be clingy and unwilling to explore the unknown. Secure kids know they have a safe place to come back to, and that if they get lost, mom or dad will come looking for them.

When we are rooted in God's love and acceptance, we have a similar sense of security, and this frees us to take risks and explore the spiritual realm because we know we aren't going to lose God's love. Our security enables us to function from that love, and empowers us to follow the leading of the Holy Spirit, whether that leading is to call someone, send a card to someone, or bless someone we don't know with a gift. We're willing to take even larger risks: commit to feeding the poor, serve the lonely at a nursing home, plant a church, volunteer for a community service agency, or work with middle schoolers in the church.

For me, being rooted in God's total acceptance has meant being free to explore topics on Sunday morning that I had previously been afraid to preach on. I no longer feel that I need to preach safe and palatable three-point sermons that have as much substance as Marshmallow Peeps; I can explore real-life issues and challenges. Sometimes I have bitten off more than the congregation or I can chew, but God's acceptance of me remains stable and unchanged, whether the message I delivered was stellar or stale.

Are you rooted in God's love? Ponder some of the biggest successes in your life. How much more did God accept you than he has at other times? Now ponder some of your biggest failures. How much less did God accept you? Would you be willing to explore more areas of your inner life if you knew God would still accept you, no matter what you found? Would you be more willing to serve others and risk rejection if you knew that you could come back to God's unchanging acceptance?

Maybe what we really need is a perspective change. Instead of defining ourselves by our achievements, things, and reputation, we need to rest secure in our identity as God's beloved children. When we do, we'll begin exploring the vast and varied world beyond the confines of our suburbic playpen.

Root Yourself in God's Prodigal Nature

Have you ever wondered why all Jelly Bellies don't taste like chicken? Life would be boring if every jelly bean we ate were bursting with a chicken essence. Currently there are fifty official Jelly Belly flavors. I can chomp on Berry Blue, Blueberry, Bubble Gum, Buttered Popcorn, Cafe Latte, Cappuccino, Chocolate Pudding, Cinnamon, Coconut, Cotton Candy, A&W Cream Soda (cream), Grape Jelly, Juicy Pear, Kiwi, Lemon, Lemon Lime, Licorice, Margarita, Peach, Peanut Butter, Piña Colada, Raspberry, A&W Root Beer, Strawberry Cheesecake, Strawberry Daiquiri, Toasted Marshmallow, Tutti-Frutti, Watermelon. . . . God created a world in which we can enjoy hundreds of nuances of flavor. Jelly Bellies are an incredible example of God's prodigal nature.

To understand what this means, we have to understand the meaning of *prodigal.*

prodigal: One who expends money extravagantly, viciously, or without necessity; one that is profuse or lavish in any expenditure; a waster; a spendthrift.[2]

If we apply this definition to the characters in the parable Jesus tells in Luke 15, then the story is not just about a prodigal son (who represents us), it is also about a prodigal father (who represents God). God and humanity both are lavish and wasteful. One in a life-stealing way and God in a life-giving way.

Notice how much love and mercy and forgiveness the father pours upon his son when the boy returns. The father's love is prodigal in every way. First, he gives his son the inheritance when the boy should have waited. Then, he never stops looking for his son, even though as a landowner he should have been working and keeping an eye on his workers. When the boy returns home, the father runs to him when he should have sternly waited on the porch. The father hugs and kisses the son, even though he smells like pigs. Instead of shaming the boy, the father clothes him with a robe and affirms his identity as his son. On and on . . .

God's prodigal nature prevents him from creating a world in which all Jelly Belly jelly beans taste like chicken. It's against God's nature to give us only one or two flavors to enjoy; that's why we enjoy hundreds of taste sensations.

I remember the first time I sipped a latte when I was visiting some friends in San Luis Obispo, California, a few decades ago. I imagine God was up in heaven, looking down on me, just waiting to see how much I enjoyed this flavor he had created. He probably even knew I'd get addicted. . . . I'm just glad my latte didn't taste like chicken. But soon it wasn't just a simple latte that I was experimenting with. Oh no, once this part of my personality was unleashed, I tried everything from the double tall French Vanilla breve with a splash of cinnamon to the triple shot Midnight Express (a triple shot, mixed with coffee and condensed milk). Ooh la la . . .

Even nature reflects God's extravagance. Whenever people from the plains states visit me, they constantly comment on how green everything is.

"Wow, I can't believe how green it is around here."

"Yep, we get a lot of rain," I respond.

"Look how green those trees are."

"Yep, they get a lot of rain."

"Check out the dark green moss hanging off those trees."

"Yep, the moss gets a lot of rain also."

"Gosh, is everyone's lawn always so green around here?"

"Yep, it even rains on our lawns around here."

What is amazing is that Washington state isn't just green. It is *greens*. I mean, we have moss green, forest green, moldy green, light green, leafy green, grass green, and on and on. We have more greens than Jelly Belly has flavors. Why? Because it is God's creative prodigal nature to not just make green. He had to create many different shades of green. Then to make the greens really look superior, he decided to make a hundred hues of yellows and reds during the fall season. Mix it with a sunset and a Margarita Jelly Belly, and you've got the perfect romantic date.

God's kingdom, by his very nature, is marked by diversity. God's communities are built by multiplicity and creativity, and kingdom spirituality seeks to be lavish and diverse in its gifts. But suburbic spirituality settles for conformity, uniformity, and efficiency.

Too many of us have convinced ourselves that we are narrow and limited in our scope of influence. For instance, take the church's use of spiritual gifts surveys, those handy little devices for getting people to step up and perform tasks at church. We take surveys, identify one or two primary gifts, and then spend the next ten years in our church communities defined by what we *were* on that given day.

But what if we have an entire fruit salad of spiritual gifts and not just a couple of slices of banana and a grape? When I go to Grandma's for Thanksgiving and dish up some fruit salad, I never know what I'm going to get. Sometimes I scoop out more grapes than peaches. Other times I scoop out more raisins than bananas. Grandma's salads have a wide variety of fruit. I can pick and choose what I want, or I can just dig in and see what lands on my plate. Either way, I know it will be good because my grandma made it.

At times God has reached into my life and pulled forth the gift of hospitality. Now hospitality isn't a gift that receives very high marks on my spiritual gifts survey, but if I looked at God and said, "What? You want me to be thoughtful and kind to our guests by doing dishes myself instead of having them help me? No, that's not my gift. You got the wrong guy. *Leadership* is my gift. . . ." God would probably use my ego to scrub the plates. I would also be failing to reflect his prodigal nature.

All of God's creation reflects his prodigal nature, including us. We are made in his image. Just as God is hospitality, so are we, and there are times when God calls us to use that gift for him. There is nothing he calls us to do that we're not equipped to handle and won't bless others. Each of us has a plethora of gifts and abilities within us, just waiting for the Creator to call them forth.

How do you root yourself in God's prodigal nature and find a whole new identity? By magnifying the Lord, as if through a magnifying glass, and taking a closer look. As you ponder God's prodigal nature in the Word, in the world around you, and through your senses, you will begin to magnify him and see this aspect of his character in everything. His abundant goodness, overwhelming creativity, and lavish love will seem to permeate every portion of your life. Next thing you know, you will have restored a sense of wonder and will no longer be a slave to routine. You will realize that you are a reflection of God's prodigal nature, and you will become more lavish in your love, compassion, generosity, and creativity because you have found your identity in him.

Root Yourself in God's Relentless Pursuit

The third God-given identity-shaper that has helped me through dark valleys has been understanding that God never gives up on me. Oh, I have often given up on God. Found myself walking away from trusting his provision, forgiveness, and wisdom. It seems more natural to trust myself than to trust Jesus. I have to *choose* to trust him with my concerns and problems; otherwise, I naturally default to me.

As crazy as it sounds, it's as natural for God to pursue us as it is for us *not* to pursue him. I love the passage in the Great Shepherd's psalm that says, "Surely goodness and love will follow me all the days of my life" (Psalm@23:6). Here, David recognizes that God's love will be with him, whether he's walking the easy street of green pastures or slogging through the valley of darkness. The Hebrew word translated here as "follow" is translated most every other place in the Old Testament as "pursue."[3] The word is a military term, as in Joshua pursuing his enemies and annihilating them. God's pursuit of us is relentless, passionate, and purposeful.

Hey, listen, God is not going to give up on you. Goodness and Mercy-Love, like sheepdogs, are nipping at your heels every time you begin to move away from God's presence and protection. He has given you free will, so you can choose whether to love him back. But regardless of the choices you have made, God is still pursuing you. Mind-boggling, isn't it? It's in God's nature to love you, to want you near.

If you are a parent, you have an inkling of what God feels for you. When one of my kids is hurt—I mean real hurt not just tattletale hurt—or in danger, I want to rescue him or her. I would go through anything to see my kids safe or free from fear, torment, pain, and disease. I've heard of parents who have gone back into burning homes without even thinking about the risk in order to rescue their children. This is a natural, healthy, loving response for a parent. Our Father in heaven is as healthy and whole as they come, and he uses his omnipotence, omniscience, and omnipresence to do whatever he can to bring us from a place of mere existence to a place of abundance.

What would happen if you and I began to choose to be as committed to our relationship with God as he is to us? What if we released the divine characteristics of faithfulness and commitment that lie dormant and subdued in our souls?

This pursuit frees us from having to choose between distractions and detours. It frees us to persevere and press through life, even when times are tough and the world is rough. God speaks to us so clearly that he is faithful to complete the work he has started. If the relentless pursuit of relationship is part of his nature, it should be a part of ours as well.

I was reminded of this the other day as I was dunkin' biscotti in a dark roast with a seeker dude who had more questions about Jesus than I had answers. But even before he signed on the "conversionary" dotted line (just kidding), he was reflecting the nature of God to me.

"Eric, even if I never really find God, I'm never going to stop looking," he said, forcing me to swallow hard instead of spitting up coffee in my excitement.

"The Jesus you ask about promises in his Book that anyone who seeks with all their heart will find him," I replied in my seriously spiritual, pastoral voice.

"No, I mean even if *you and I* never find all of him, we should not stop looking."

Hey, how'd I get pulled into this conversion?

But he was right. Just like God never stops, never gives up, never falters in his love and pursuit of us, we can find our very identities when we do the same in our relationship with him. People often ask me if my church is a seeker-oriented church. I respond, "I guess so. I'm the pastor and I'm still seeking."

Thanks, seeker dude, for another revelation.

Are you fixated on the transient ever-changing opinions of others and on trying to improve your position in life? Don't spend your time, talent, and treasures trying to grab hold of the wind. Instead, lay down your desire to get your identity from others, from institutions, and culture, and get it straight from your Creator instead.

▸STOP, ▸LOOK, & LISTEN

1. Do you remember what your five senses are? (If not, ask your elementary-aged nephew.) Take one sense per hour today and write down as many sensations as you can that reflect God's prodigal nature.

2. This is a cool way to evaluate the distance your life feels from God. Get a United States map. Pretend God is in Washington, DC, and that Hollywood, California, is the city farthest away from God. (The opposite may be more true.) Where are you on the map?

- Evaluate your distance from God.
- Then look around the landscape of your life. Is God doing anything right now to nip at your heels? How are you responding?
- Do you see a road to take you where you want to go?

CHAPTER THREE

A PROMISING CAREER

On Calling

I'M A MOVIE GUY. The local cable station, TNT, even has a weekly movie in my honor. Friday nights from 8 to10 p.m. they show "movies for guys who like movies." They fill this time slot with great guy movies—movies in which lots of things get blown up . . . or a hero rises from obscurity . . . or a beautiful girl needs to be rescued . . . or some ripped, butt-kicking action hero takes on twenty bad guys all at once while simultaneously pulling an arrow out of his leg. Ahh, movies for guys who like movies. I love it.

My wife, Cindy, doesn't get it. She'd rather watch some poignant, emotional story of two people falling in and out love four times before I can even microwave a bag of popcorn. Of course, while they schmooze each other, the characters must simultaneously wrestle with some horrid issue from their childhood or discover a secret so wrenching that it can only be solved with the help of an entire box of Kleenex. I don't get it, . . . but Cindy and I keep another night set aside just for her that we affectionately like to call "movies for guys who have to watch chick flicks with their wives" night.

I realize that one reason for our different movie preferences has to do with how guys and gals are hardwired. But gender isn't the only factor. Both my wife and my best friend, Wayne, resonate with characters who work through their life struggles with an intimate other, with characters who go beyond gunshot wounds into heart and soul wounds and come out healed. Cindy and Wayne are wired to be compassionate and empathic. (*Hmm . . . what does that say about me?*) My wife has this incredible ability to take people who are struggling with life hurts, embrace them and their pain, and then help them find healing. Of course, this kind of commitment takes more of her time than a 120-minute movie, and much more than a single box of Kleenex.

Now, mind you, I'm not cold and insensitive. I've been known to shed tears into my large buttered popcorn. Granted, I seldom get emotional during chick flicks, even with all the estrogen in the air, but I can cry nonetheless:

- I cried during *Armageddon* when the astronauts landed and the little boy ran out on the tarmac to greet his hero father.
- I cried while viewing *The Last Samurai* as the two men who were once enemies fought together and died as friends.
- I cried when the kid in *Pay It Forward* ultimately gave his life doing what he believed in.
- I even sprinkled a few tears during *The Gladiator* when Maximus finally had his vow fulfilled, even though it cost him his life.

Still, few movies have captured my emotions and provided me with such a transcendent experience as the *Lord of the Rings* trilogy. Why? Because these films present a powerful picture of what it means to live out one's calling.

At the close of the *Return of the King*, Frodo and Sam are struggling to climb Mount Doom. They are so close to their destination, but Frodo has reached the point of exhaustion. Sam, his lifelong friend and companion, says: "I may not be able to carry the ring, but I can carry you." With every bit of strength he has left, Sam stands up, puts Frodo over his shoulders, and begins the final ascent to fulfill the destiny for which they were created. I'm sitting in the theater, watching this powerful scene, and I suddenly begin sobbing like a girl watching *Divine Secrets of the Ya-Ya Sisterhood*. Pass the paper napkins; I gotta blow my nose . . .

My friend Sonny, who was watching the movie with me, also had a strong emotional response at the same point in the movie. He identified with faithful Sam, who likes being in the background, even though he is as committed as Frodo to destroying the ring of power. Sam didn't bear the burden of the ring; he bore the burden of the ring bearer. Powerful stuff for Sonny, because as a servant leader, he saw himself in Sam.

I, on the other hand, deeply identified with Frodo, the reluctant hero. Not just because we are both short, but also because Frodo often struggled with feeling that, although he had clearly been given the task of destroying the ring, the job was too big for him to accomplish. Frodo was doing what he was *called* to do, and whenever he was about to fail, "destiny" had someone or something help him fulfill his calling.

Most of us hunger for something greater and more meaningful than what our jobs or responsibilities offer us. I suspect this is why we so often escape into the transcendent world provided by our fifty-two-inch, flat screen, home movie theater systems. We are trying to feed our souls through the lives of celluloid characters, but the satisfaction of the screen is short-lived.

However, God doesn't want us to live vicariously through mythical characters like Frodo, or even through biblical characters like Joshua or Esther. He wants us to live our own story, in the here and now. He wants us to persevere *like* Frodo persevered, to trust him *like* Joshua trusted him, and to risk obedience *like* Esther risked obedience.

Gandalf said to Frodo, "All you have to do is decide what to do with the time given to you."

The Lord said to Joshua, "As I was with Moses, so I will be with you; I will never leave you nor forsake you. Be strong and courageous, because you will lead these people" (Joshua@1:5-6).

Mordecai said to Esther, "And who knows but that you have come to royal position for such a time as this" (Esther@4:14).

When I read these statements, they speak into my soul and shake loose my desire to follow Jesus wherever he may lead. They invite me out of suburbia, into the adventure of living out my calling.

The Road to Calling

I've come to believe that God is constantly speaking to us through our culture. He speaks to us through the multiplicity of media, knowing that we will relate to certain characters in movies, literature, or the Bible. Through that connection, he brings forth something within us that has been lying dormant for far too long. Like the pull of a magnet, our hearts are drawn toward a place or a person or a passion. As we move toward that pull, the attraction becomes stronger. We can't see the charged ions floating around, but we definitely can feel the effects of them.

Calling is something that comes from *within* us. Perhaps the following story will help explain what I mean. I used to work with developmentally delayed children in my university's child development center. One child in particular, Jonah, had a disorder that kept him from engaging with the other children and almost exclusively locked him into his own little imaginative world. We constantly were looking for ways to connect with Jonah. Hand signals, gentle nudges, and picture books just didn't seem to get his attention. Then one day, I was sitting next to him while playing telephone with another child. The play phone rang, and before I could pick it up to say "hello," Jonah grabbed it and said, "Hello, this is Jonah." I was stunned. Apparently the ringing of the telephone triggered something within him, and he responded.

Something similar happens when we are exposed to our God-given calling, whether it comes in the form of a sound, a character in a movie or book, or an opportunity. We are living our mundane lives, focused on our own little worlds, and then suddenly something inside us leaps and yells, "Hello!"

But if we're not careful, our other responsibilities can disconnect that call and force us back to living life the way we have always lived it. So many of us have settled for spiritual suburbia. It's much easier to take the path of least resistance and follow the roadmap on how to read the Bible in a year (understanding is optional), give intellectual assent to four basic laws of Christiandom (heartfelt change is optional), and pay our church tithe (this is required to stay in good standing). Before we know it, we're cruising the roads of comfortable Christianity well into our retirement years.

But I ask you, where's the adventure in that? Where's the reality in that?

Jesus tells us that the road to life is narrow and few actually find it. Yes, he is referring to *eternal life*, but could he also be talking about *this* life? Could he also be saying that we can know we are in the right place at the right time, in the here and now? I believe he is. I believe Jesus is telling us that we can walk in abundant peace, abundant fulfillment, abundant grace, and abundant life *right now*. After all, just a few verses before he was talking about asking and receiving from God: "How much more will your Father in heaven give good gifts to those who ask him!" (Matthew@7:11).

So, Jesus, I'm asking. Show me my call. I'm listening. . . .

I don't know about you, but just doing the right things and behaving the right way is not what I signed up for. I want to know fulfillment and purpose in all I set my hands to — I want to do what I'm called by God to do.

Before we get to how we can do this, let's take a look at a couple of reasons why some of us never pursue our God-given calling and remain stuck in spiritual suburbia.

▸STOP, ▸LOOK, & LISTEN

What is God saying to *you*? Have you found yourself trying to live out your calling through movies, or books like the *Left Behind* series, or even through the great stories of mighty men and women of faith? *Or* are those characters propelling you forward into the future God has called you to live?

Wearing Someone Else's Shirt

My friend Rob is one brilliant guy. He has a PhD in chemistry from the University of California at San Diego. After he got his degree, he spent a few years in a job for a major chemical company before he realized that he was in a career that wasn't his calling. His calling was to heal the sick, so he quit his high-paying, *Dexter's Laboratory*-type job and went to Harvard and got a MD in internal medicine. Like I said—the guy is brilliant.

Not long ago, I was wearing a Harvard sweatshirt that I had purchased at a Goodwill thrift store for $3.99. Someone asked me, "Wow, did you go to Harvard?" I wanted so badly to live vicariously through Rob, and to substitute my name into his credits. Instead, I told the truth. Obviously, the person was no longer impressed.

Still the whole episode got me thinking about how many jerseys and sweatshirts I wear that represent other people's callings.

- On Monday I could be Hall-of-Famer John Elway, #7 of the Denver Broncos.
- On Tuesday I could be Ichiro batting for the Seattle Mariners.
- On Wednesday I could be back on the Broncos with the Super Bowl XXXVIII sweatshirt that I got at Wal-Mart.
- On Thursday you could find me filling in for Richard Petty driving for NASCAR.
- On Friday and Saturday I'm back on the Broncos (I'm sure Raiders' fans have stopped reading this book by now.).
- On Sunday I'm serving on God's team with any number of sweatshirts.

But what is it that God has called me to do? Am I only wearing someone else's shirt and not living the life God has for me? Do I wear the shirts because I want to be associated with a champion or a hero or a success story? You see, Rob can wear his Harvard *or* his UCSD sweatshirts with authenticity because he went to those institutions in order to fulfill his calling. He put out beaucoup (uh, boo-coo) bucks to pay for that privilege. His is a story of a man pursuing his calling.

Christians who are living in spiritual suburbia "just wear the shirt." We often profess to be "followers of Christ," but are we really following him into what he has called us to do? Are we fulfilling our unique, God-given purpose? It's possible to say all the right words, yet never surrender our hearts and wills to God's leading. God wants us to live out our calling; he doesn't just want us to wear his shirt.

Nor does he want us to live by default.

Serving by Default

One of the great dangers of living in spiritual suburbia is the temptation to enjoy the stability of a consistent paycheck, which provides us with "things," but at the cost of fulfilling our God-given calling. We don't believe that God has more for us. Some of us believe that calling is only for pastors, missionaries, and turbo-charged Christians. Some of us don't believe we can make a difference. Some have bought the lie that calling is only for the skilled and seminary-trained. Some of us believe that calling is only a hyper-spiritual way of talking about church duty. And so we live life by default, often doing good things.

Churches always have more needs than resources. They have less money and more expenses . . . less teachers and more kids in need of teaching . . . less home group leaders and more people who need to be plugged in to a home group . . . more building maintenance problems and less volunteers who can fix them. Oh, how easy it is for leaders to see the people as commodities that exist to serve the machine called "church," regardless of whether the job fits their calling or not.

Because of this, many Christians are doing acts of service in the church, but they aren't following their calling. They happened into their church just when the church needed a youth leader or Sunday school teacher or nursery worker, so for the next ten years that's the role they fulfill. At least until they get a glimpse of their real calling, and then they break down the fences of church suburbia and say, "No. God's told me to feed the poor."

How simple it is to serve by default, and not just in things we do at church. We can live by default in our jobs or careers and in our volunteer activities. We get a job and work our tails off just to stay afloat financially, and may even try our best to do some good things for God in the process. But we never become fully alive in our souls because we never fully become what God has created us to be.

We sense that God has something deeper for us. That we were created for something more, but often the weight of responsibility presses us down and buries that nagging sense of dissatisfaction and the hope of something more. So we settle into the safety of the good things we are already doing, and build a fence around it to keep it contained.

But what if? . . . What if we took a risk and explored who we were created to be? What if we grabbed life by purpose and not by default? What if we sought a calling instead of simply earning a living?

Grabbing Life by Purpose

Remember, calling comes from *within*, not from others telling us what our calling is. When we live out our calling, we sense that we are fulfilling our purpose, that we are in the *right place* at the *right time*. In the poetic words of Eugene Peterson, living out of our calling is "moving to the rhythms of God's grace."[1]

Few of us discover our calling just by accident. Most of the time we only find it if we look for it and pursue it. But because calling comes from within, we can't just take some personality or spiritual gifts survey and— *voila!*—identify our calling. Until we get our hearts right, we will continually misfire on how we express our calling. Nor can we just drop all our responsibilities and routines, like we are in some spiritual midlife crisis. In order to find our calling, we must explore and risk believing that, "We are God's workmanship, created in Christ Jesus to do good works, which God prepared in advance for us to do" (Ephesians@2:10).

▸STOP, ▸LOOK, & LISTEN

Just wearing the shirt: Draw a picture of a T-shirt or sweatshirt representing each of the different roles you fulfill during the week (parent, friend, pizza delivery person, choir singer, and so on). Try to identify shirts that you wear that really don't fit you on the inside, but look good on you from the outside. Are there shirts you must wear but that need new purpose and passion breathed into them? Are there some shirts you wish you could wear but you haven't taken the time to truly earn the privilege of wearing?

Ask God to Speak to You

I remember my own struggle to find my calling. I was just rounding the last furlough of my doctorate degree from Oregon State University (at least I can wear *that* sweatshirt). I was still instructing Human Sexuality and Child Development courses for the university, while Cindy worked part-time on a tech support line for Hewlett Packard and full-time as a new mother. My doctoral course work was completed, and my final written exams were approaching. I knew that my academic journey was coming to a close. Now what? Cindy and I knew we were at an important crossroads. I didn't know what to do or where to apply.

We did not want to just take a job by default or drift through the years of our lives. Some things were clear. Cindy felt that one of her callings was to be a stay-at-home mom. Her desire had always been, and continued to be, pulled toward investing in our young daughter (and later our son). And I knew that one of my callings was to put my marriage and family first. The career path I chose had to be in harmony with that call. Did God have other callings for me to live out?

One of the challenges of discovering our calling is that it's often plural and not singular. We shouldn't hang up our primary callings (our friendship with Jesus, our marriage and/or family), while we answer the line for a newer, more glamorous calling. Maybe that's why we have call waiting. . . .

So Cindy and I took the most important step toward discovering a call: prayer. We took the time to ask God to speak to us. In the midst of the whirlwind of options, we wanted to hear God's voice in a whisper.

I interviewed for what I considered my dream job—

a position with Focus on the Family. I prayed and hoped they wanted a disillusioned sex professor on their staff, even if it was just to sweep floors or mow the lawn. In the meantime, a couple universities were flirting with me about becoming a full-time professor, and I kept seeing those USA Truck Driving Academy commercials on late night television. Every job I looked at appealed to me in some way.

Pursue God's Presence Most of All

During that time of indecisive insomnia, my devotions brought me to Numbers 9, and to what have to be the most redundant eight verses in the Bible. But read it and read it slowly . . .

> On the day the tabernacle, the Tent of the Testimony, was set up, the cloud covered it. From evening till morning the cloud above the tabernacle looked like fire. That is how it continued to be; the cloud covered it, and at night it looked like fire. Whenever the cloud lifted from above the Tent, the Israelites set out; wherever the cloud settled, the Israelites encamped. At the LORD's command the Israelites set out, and at his command they encamped. As long as the cloud stayed over the tabernacle, they remained in camp. When the cloud remained over the tabernacle a long time, the Israelites obeyed the LORD's order and did not set out. Sometimes the cloud was over the tabernacle only a few days; at the LORD's command they would encamp, and then at his command they would set out. Sometimes the cloud stayed only from evening till morning, and when it lifted in the morning, they set out. Whether by

day or by night, whenever the cloud lifted, they set out. Whether the cloud stayed over the tabernacle for two days or a month or a year, the Israelites would remain in camp and not set out; but when it lifted, they would set out. At the LORD's command they encamped, and at the LORD's command they set out. They obeyed the LORD's order, in accordance with his command through Moses. (Numbers@9:15-23)

It doesn't take a seminary degree to see a pattern in these verses. Do you think God is trying to make a point? First, there is the cloud. The cloud of smoke (and the pillar of fire by night) symbolizes the presence of God. Second, there are the people of God. They seemed compelled to follow his presence. Third, they are in the *wilderness*. The Israelites did not know where they were or where they were going! All they could do was follow God. Where they were going wasn't important. What was important to them was that I AM was with them. They never knew how long God was going to settle, but when he did, they did.

When I read this passage, the lights suddenly went on. My predicament was similar to that of the Israelites. There I was, wandering in the wilderness of calling. I saw numerous options, but had no idea which way to go. Like that Hebrew tribe of old, I also had a choice. To pursue God's presence, or to stay in the comfort of what my wife and I had built around us. God's presence or my comfort? An easy choice on paper, but my emotions and my commitments seemed to swing toward whatever seemed to be carrying the most weight in my life at that given moment.

I had to decide that God's presence was more important

than a job title, status, or income, because if I wasn't living in his presence, I could never live out my calling, let alone find it. I had to say, "Okay, God. I'll follow you. Even if the decision is not logical."

If you can relate to my experience, if you are having trouble focusing on the presence of God or knowing if what you are feeling led to is of God, or if it is something else, I invite you to pray this daily prayer, penned by Thomas Merton, a man who really seemed to know God's voice. He refused to live his life in spiritual suburbia and was constantly following the presence of God and discovering new perspectives on life and love:

> My Lord God, I have no idea where I am going. I do not see the road ahead of me. I cannot know for certain where it will end. Nor do I really know myself, and the fact that I think that I am following your will does not mean that I am actually doing so.
>
> But I believe that the desire to please you does in fact please you. And I hope I have that desire in all that I am doing. I hope that I will never do anything apart from that desire. And I know that if I do this you will lead me by the right road though I may know nothing about it.
>
> Therefore will I trust you always though I may seem to be lost and in the shadow of death. I will not fear, for you are ever with me, and you will never leave me to face my perils alone.[2]

When we pray a prayer like this, we keep our hearts open to God's leading and our faith anchored to his sovereignty. In praying this prayer we submit our wills and our future to God's goodness and not our logic.

▸STOP, & LISTEN
▸LOOK,

1. When was the last time you really enjoyed a task or act of service and sensed the presence of God about you?

2. When was the last time you performed an unpleasant task or act of service but sensed the presence of God?

3. Where is the presence of God in your life right now? Theologically we know he is present, but how about experientially? Have you asked him to be?

Do What God Tells You to Do

So there I was, still in the Wilderness of Wondering, but wanting the presence of God more than anything else—even if it meant Cindy and I would never leave the wilderness. I could sense a rumbling beginning to occur, but I had no idea what that meant, until I was sitting in a bar, drinking coffee, and studying for my exams in the rural town of Port Angeles, Washington.

I had asked an old friend who lived there if I could spend a couple days with him, just so I could get out of town and study. It was a six-hour drive, but the distance was worth the limited distractions his small town would provide me. There, I could study social psychology theories, bend my brain around statistical measures and formulas, and get ready to pretend I was a whole lot smarter than I was come testing time. What I didn't expect was to drift into God's pillar of fire.

For some reason I was reading (actually I was scanning), through the book of Leviticus when a passage seemed to jump out at me. Leviticus 10 tells the story of Aaron's two sons getting a bit tanked up on the local brew and then going and burning an unauthorized fire for God. God wasn't happy, and so the fire consumed them, right there on the spot.

But that isn't what caught my attention. What caught my attention was that Aaron remained silent. No doubt he was a bit intimidated by what he had just seen and was in shock. Moses, Aaron's brother, had the bodies carried away and then made this strange statement to Aaron, "Do not let your hair become unkempt, and do not tear your clothes, or you will die and the LORD will be angry with the whole community . . . because the LORD's anointing oil is on you" (Leviticus@10:6-7). In essence Moses is telling his brother, "Look, I know you just watched your two kids get flame-broiled, but don't mourn for them or God is going to kill you too."

At first glance, this seems cold-blooded. But the phrase that grabbed me was, "because the LORD's anointing oil is on you." According to this passage, God had anointed Aaron for a specific task, and God wanted him to fulfill that call before Aaron got on with his own personal business. Later, Aaron does get to take care of his sons' funerals, but at this moment his brother is reminding him that he was anointed to be a priest, and that he had to fulfill that calling first.

It was then that the Shekinah glory hit me. At least, I think that's what it was, because suddenly in the midst of that smoke-filled bar, I had an overwhelming sense of excitement, fear, hope, and insecurity at the same time. I wish I could tell you that an apparition of Monica from *Touched by an Angel* or some version of God from *Joan of Arcadia* appeared and said she had a message from God for me. Or that a choir of heavenly hosts suddenly cranked up the karaoke machine and sang a song of calling for me. Nope, it was much more subtle and fuzzy.

I just sensed Wisdom saying, "Eric, you can do all kinds of things and be fruitful. But you have always sensed that I have called you to full-time ministry. My presence for you is here in Port Angeles. Come plant a church." It was as if the Holy Spirit himself was telling me, "This is what I've made you for." I knew that God wanted me to plant a church in Port Angeles, Washington. This anointing was also my calling.

So that's what I did. For the first time in many years, my wife and I both felt like we were in the right place at the right time in our lives, even when it got tough.

When we follow God's calling, all the pieces come together to reveal the glory and purpose of God in our lives. Sometimes we're anointed for a season, sometimes for a lifetime. But when it happens, the comfort and predictability of redundancy give way to the adventure and passion of intentionality.

So calling is less about *what* you do, and more about *who you are*. Just because I didn't end up at Focus on the Family doesn't mean that those who do work there are not called. Just because I don't teach at a university doesn't mean all professors aren't called to teach. It just means I wasn't called to that place at that time in *my* story. To paraphrase what John Wimber, founder of the Vineyard Church movement, said, "We are all just God's pocket change. The honor is not in what he spends us on, but in the fact that he chooses to spend us."

Of course, when you surrender to your calling, God may not only lead you on some adventuresome roads, where you'll get a God's-eye-view of humanity, he may also lead you down some rocky roads, through the valley of disillusionment and despair. Following your calling doesn't guarantee the three Ps of success as defined by suburbia (popularity, prosperity, and personality). Its only guarantee is that we will be fulfilling our created purpose.

I know what some of you are thinking right now. *That's great, Eric. You grew up with a clear sense of your calling, but what about those of us who came to Jesus later in life, or just don't have a clear sense of what God might be calling us to do? How can we figure out our calling?*

That, my friend, is what God is inviting you to explore while continually pursuing his presence. Your calling is the uncharted territory where you must push the limits of what you have known so that you can move into the center of God's will for your life.

God isn't likely to work the same way in your life as he does in mine, so I'm not going to tell you to do it "my way." He may reveal your calling to you in a completely different way. You need to explore the smoke, the mist, and the mystery of the presence of God yourself. Pray Merton's prayer, be willing to take some risks, and solidify your spiritual foundations. God will write your calling on your heart when it is time. And when he does, you will know.

But don't wait passively for some out-of-body experience.

Wait Aggressively

As my friend and mentor, Marty Schaffer, taught me, wait aggressively. What does this mean? Do everything you know to do at this time and place in your life. Some things are just obvious when it comes to being a follower of Christ. Honor your marriage vows, love and invest in your kids, develop a heart of worship. Other things are equally important: Feed the poor, care for the sick, build up the body of Christ, stand against injustice, mentor and make disciples. . . . You get the idea.

Waiting aggressively means not walking away from responsibilities, but purposing to keep in harmony with the will and Word of God. Pride, fear, and comfort often keep us from experimenting. Experimenting often enables us to discover the callings that are lying dormant within us.

Don't go "oughto-matic" either. *I ought to do this; I ought to do that. . . .* I once knew a woman who functioned this way. She was so busy doing good things for her church that she was only serving her children halfway. The voices in her head said she ought to be at the women's Bible study, although her daughter wanted her to be a classroom aid. The voices in her head said she ought to practice with the worship team, although her kids wanted her help with their homework. The voices in her head said she ought to live in a nicer house and keep her full-time job so they could afford the nice home, although her heart said she needed to be home with her kids after school.

This woman couldn't clearly hear what God had called her to because she was focusing on all she "ought to" do. So she took some time to question everything and wait aggressively. She went back to what was most important to her—pursuing the presence of God in her life. She cried out, "God, you are what I wanted from the very beginning. Pull my life back into the story you have for me."

That decision led her to follow the heart that God gave her, not the heart Wal-Mart offered her. It was then that she came alive in her calling to be a neighborhood mom. She not only made herself available to her own kids, she was available for her kids' friends as well. She found herself in the right place at the right time—at home with her children.

So don't listen to your "ought tos," to find your calling. Instead, submit every "yes" and "no," every "ought to" and "should," to Jesus the Master, not just Fred the pastor. As you slow down to do only those things that seem right to you and the Holy Spirit, you may find that you are already walking in your calling.

You may come to rediscover God's purpose in what you *are already doing.* You may become convinced that God has indeed called you to the career you are in, the job you have, or the roles you are currently engaged in. If this is the case, and yet you still feel as if you have been living in spiritual suburbia, the way out is by stumbling forward and pairing up with a good mentor.

▶STOP, ▶LOOK, & LISTEN

1. Wait aggressively. What would that look like in your life right now? Which part of that phrase is the most difficult for you: waiting or being aggressive?

2. Better to be good at a few things than mediocre at a bunch of things. Does this sentence speak to your life? Are there a few "ought tos" that you could erase from your life in order to enhance the "goods"?

Find a Good Mentor

The summer prior to my senior year in high school, our football coach, Doc, gathered his testosterone-laden team around and began to assign positions for the season-opening game. When he got to punt returner, he said my name, and the team let out a collective moan. You see, I was a decent tailback and defensive safety, but when it came to returning punts, I had about as much success holding on to the football as a kid chasing a greased pig.

But ol' Doc wouldn't take no for an answer. Instead, he had

me stay after practice for the rest of the pre-season so he could punt footballs to me. He would punt; I would drop. He would punt; I would drop. I would beg to be released from the burden; then he would punt another, and I would drop another.

After a week or two of this, something began to change. Perhaps it was *his* belief in my ability, coupled with the relentless repetition of after-practice dropping sessions, but just in time for the season opener, I began to catch the darn thing consistently. And you know what? I actually went from zero to hero over the course of that football season. Thanks to some patient coaching, I became an all-state punt returner, and learned the lifelong lesson of the power of having a good mentor.

So did Samuel. His ability to hear God's voice and walk in his calling as a prophet provided him quite a reputation. He even held a remarkable conversation with God while simultaneously being the only judge for the "Mr. King of Israel" pageant (see 1 Samuel 16). But Samuel wasn't always good at hearing God's voice—which is an important skill for someone who is called to be a prophet, wouldn't you say? Early on in his life, he wasn't able to discern between God's voice and his mentor, Eli's. Eli helped Samuel learn how to trust both voices, and to live out his calling.

If you discover that you are in your calling, but not walking in it successfully, you may need to find a mentor who can help you do so. Is there someone whom you can trust to see what God is doing in you or wants to do through you? Find a person who genuinely has the voice of the Good Shepherd. They are out there.

You may have to explore a bit more and get outside of your preconceived spiritual hierarchy to find them. Often they are cloistered in the prayer closets or relegated to serving where the spotlights don't shine. But I am convinced that every community of faith has folks whose calling is mentoring others. And you will know you have found such a person when he or she is more concerned with your character than with your gifts.

It may be that living out your calling and developing your career are the same thing. Or it may be that in order to walk in your calling, you'll have to give up the security of a regular paycheck or the status of a name plaque on your desk. Leaving spiritual suburbia means laying down our lives for the sake of the gospel, which may require laying down our livelihoods. As Jesus leads, we must follow. Are you willing?

▸STOP, ▸LOOK, & LISTEN

1. Can you recall times in your life that you were mentored and not just managed? What made the difference?

2. Are you willing to take risks in your calling and fail? If you do fail, how do you feel failure would impact God's commitment and love toward you? How about your mentor's commitment and love toward you?

3. This might be fun. Get some paper and a pencil. Draw a map representing your current suburbia and the unexplored land of your calling. Why did you make the landscape the way you did? Ask the Holy Spirit to show you where you are in the journey toward your calling.

CHAPTER FOUR

A TELEVISION IN EVERY ROOM

On Doubt and Discouragement

SILENCE USED TO SCARE me. Not Freddie-Kruger-horror-movie scared. No, my fear of silence was a much more unsettling fear, similar to the fear I felt as a kid in an unfamiliar place in the dark. When my world was silent, thoughts would creep into my head from every direction, so I'd turn on the television to keep those thoughts at bay. Some things I just didn't want to think about.

Apparently, I'm not alone in this. According to sociological statistics, the average American watches over four hours of television per day.[1] Since I'm a pretty average guy, that means by the time I turn sixty-five, I will have spent nine years of my life marinating in the glow of the tube. Of course, many of us just watch television for the educational programming, right? Wrong. Much of the time, we're watching to distract our souls.

When we live in spiritual suburbia, we spend a lot of time distracting ourselves in order to keep from thinking about the things we don't want to think about, such as the annoying little gremlin called Doubt and the fast-growing beast known as Discouragement. Maybe our distraction is simply a form of denial. Maybe our pretending happens because we don't know or don't like who we really are. Regardless, we keep ourselves so busy, so preoccupied with things that don't really matter, that real growth and real life gets stymied. Ironically, ignoring doubt and discouragement only feeds them, while facing them head-on crushes them and turns them into fertilizer for our faith.

In spiritual suburbia it's easy to start pretending and to stop growing, to distract ourselves with things happening outside of us so that we can neglect the things inside of us. I know this first-hand.

The Distraction of God's Army

Back in my university days, I had the opportunity to attend a spiritual retreat for a nationwide campus ministry. Situated high in the Rocky Mountains, the gathering took place at the magnificent YMCA camp in Estes Park, Colorado. Due to its size, the YMCA can host numerous organizations simultaneously. As fate would have it, my seventy-five campus ministry cronies shared cafeteria space with a large contingent of Army ROTC (Reserve Officer Training Corps) weekend warriors.

Both groups dressed in their appropriate soldier's uniforms. The ROTC gang sported camouflage pants and shirts and shiny, black boots. Their attire almost made them invisible next to the salad bar. Of course everyone in my group, God's little army, fired up after listening to the evangelist-warrior speaker guy, had our custom-sheathed swords (Bibles) at our sides as well as various-sized medallions of our Commander hanging around our necks. There was no doubt we were Christians. If you couldn't tell by our uniforms, you could surely tell by the conversations that saturated our cafeteria table.

"Praise the Lord. I am so stoked to take our campus for Jesus!"

"Amen, brother. Just look at what it says here in . . . in . . . well I don't know where it is, but the Bible says that Jesus wants us to make disciples of everyone we meet."

"Yep, we are leaving here as God's army. Pass the mustard." (That was my contribution.)

Suddenly, our conversation was drowned out by the disrespectful comments of the ROTC guys sitting at the table behind us. They were totally disin' Christ and making fun of the fact that we felt compelled to bring our swords to the cafeteria with us. Then it happened. One of them made a statement that caused the great defender of the faith to rise up within me. They actually used God's name in vain.

"Excuse me," I told my comrades as I pushed away from my table and went to sit down in the Enemy's camp.

Feeling lawyer-like, kinda like Tom Cruise in *A Few Good Men,* I sat down to boldly proclaim my faith to these insensitive heathens. However, as I began to look beyond the differences in our uniforms, I noticed these guys were real human beings. I started talking with them and discovered we had a lot in common. Like me, most of them also attended a state university and were trying to fit in extra-curricular activities (mine was ministry, theirs combat training) at the cost of studying for exams. We all loved a good pizza and movie night with our friends. Our conversation turned slowly from animosity to shared experiences. Then from shared experiences to faith experiences. We ventured back to their dorm room and talked for another hour or so.

"Christianity is okay. But I just don't get how you can profess to believe something with so many make-believe stories in it," touted Sergeant Bob.

"Make believe? The Bible is the inerrant and infallible Word of God," I protested, feeling the lawyer spirit rise up within me again. Honestly, I had no idea what those words meant. But the evangelist-warrior speaker guy had used them at the previous night's session, and they did feel powerful when I said them.

"Well what about Noah's ark? Come on. A big boat, two of every animal in the world getting on board? A flood that kills everyone? You really believe this is a true story?"

"Or how about the Jerry guy that marched around the great wall of China and blew a trumpet to knock it down?" piped in Lt. Mayberry.

"Well, actually that was Joshua, and he marched around Jericho seven times, and then they blew trumpets to knock down the wall of the city," I responded.

"Oh. *That's* more believable," quipped Commander Cody.

I was beginning to feel a bit pinned down. "Listen, there are still many things I don't know. But I can tell you my story. I can tell you how God changed my life," I said.

So I told them my story, and God used it to reach these men. Four of the six prayed a prayer to get their lives right with God. The fifth said he was an Italian Orthodox Catholic and needed to ask his grandma. The sixth guy just listened. What a powerful evening it turned out to be. Still, I came away with a little seed of doubt planted in my soul.

After scolding me for missing the evening session, because our campus ministry had paid good money to bring this evangelist-warrior guy in to speak on how to lead people to Christ, my spiritual captain addressed my concerns about Noah and Jerry.

"Don't question the Word of God. Do what you know to

do, and the rest will follow."

His words sounded so confident and sure that for the next few months I did just that. I maintained my good Christian confidence. I stayed involved in my good Christian activities, and didn't mention Noah or Jerry again. Sometimes the good things others expect us to accomplish can be the enemy of what God wants us to learn.

In the evenings, as I lay in bed, the nagging questions would arise. I would turn on late night TV and put myself to sleep with the *Twilight Zone.* Nothing like a good black-and-white retro show to provide distraction. It worked pretty well, and a pattern developed. I kept myself busy during the day and distracted myself to sleep at night. I did this for months until one time I couldn't stand it any longer, and I actually prayed. *God, forgive me for doubting your Word. But there are some things I just don't get. Like the whole Noah's ark thing. And Jerry, I mean Joshua. Is that stuff really true? I mean is it believable? I'm sorry for doubting you. Amen.*

The next day, my roommate gave me a Bible verse. Not something he was prone to doing, but that morning, over a bowl of Grape Nuts, he felt compelled. "Hey Eric, check this verse out. For some reason I wrote it out for you last night."

He handed me a slip of paper that simply said, "For wisdom will enter your heart, and knowledge will be pleasant to your soul" (Proverbs@2:10).

Amazing! God had heard my prayer! I realized that it wasn't like God was up in heaven, scratching his head wondering how he was going to explain this whole Noah thing to Eric. God knew just how wisdom could enter my heart. He knew just how much knowledge I would need to be able to walk in a stronger and more stable sense of faith.

Increased faith doesn't happen instantaneously. No, for most of us it happens as we listen and as we make space for God to speak. Doubt is like fog. It's thick and blurs our vision. But regardless, God gives us his charts (the Bible) and his guidance (the Holy Spirit) to navigate through it. What the Enemy wants us to do is abandon ship. But if we resist that urge and press in toward our doubt, our doubt will dissipate and give way to belief.

Now the space or focus of this book does not allow for the disentanglement of the God-allowed doubt that I experienced over the following weeks. What you need to know is that if God can help me navigate through the fog of doubt, he can do the same for you. For me, it started with a *National Geographic* video special on Noah's ark that my mother just *happened* to send me (she always seems to know when I need something), and it ended with a sermon series my pastor called "The Life of Noah."

Once I stopped feeding doubt with distractions, God had room to deal with my soul. I came out of the process with a stronger faith in his Word and a deeper understanding of his story than I ever had before. By distracting myself from doubt, I had also been distracting myself from God's desire to teach me that he is reliable and faithful, even when I can't see two feet in front of me.

God spoke to me so clearly through that experience that you would think I would never neglect my inner life again. Not.

Years pass and the mountaintop encounter with God dims. We get caught up in life and in our roles, and we lose sight of who we really are. Then one day, we wake up and wonder if we've just been kidding ourselves. At least that's the way it's been for me.

The Distraction of Pretending with Jesus

I once worked at an early childhood center at Colorado State University. While outside playing, a four-year-girl came running over to me. Her voice was shrill, and terror filled her eyes. Little beads of sweat had formed on her forehead. "Teacher, teacher!" she yelled as she grabbed my hand to pull me away.

"The building's on fire! The building's on fire!"

"Where, Sara? Where?" I responded, searching the playground for signs of smoke.

Tears started to well up in her eyes, "Around the corner, by the tire tunnel!"

My heart started racing as she pulled me across the playground to show me the fire. Then the snack bell rang and little Sara dropped my hand and skipped toward the door, singing the Barney song. One of her little monster cohorts grabbed my hand and asked, "Do you want to play firehouse with us next recess?"

Pretending may be okay for children, but it's not okay for adults, particularly when it comes to matters of faith. That's why I felt so unnerved one Sunday morning.

As the steam disappeared from the mirror, I found myself staring at someone who I wasn't sure I knew. The guy in the mirror had a freshly shaved face, a couple of shiny-new earrings, and, thanks to his new Sonic Care toothbrush, pearly-white teeth. But underneath my cutting-edge, metrosexual, emergent pastor image was a sewer of doubt, bringing a stench to my spiritual air.

Here I was, asking myself, "Am I even saved?" Not a good way for a pastor to start a Sunday morning. I couldn't say I truly believed anymore. God felt like an imaginary friend. My son had his stuffed Grover doll, my daughter had her Polly Pockets, and I had what felt like a plastic Jesus. My kids could invite three or four friends over to play house or Sesame Street, and I thought that was cute. But I had invited two hundred friends to come over and play church in two hours — and that stressed me out. I felt like a total pretender. Like Agent Mulder of the *X-Files*, I cried out, "I want to believe!"

God seemed so distant, so make-believe. Had my mind just been playing tricks on me all these years? I was trying hard to maintain the appearance expected of me, so no one would notice the fear and unbelief brewing within. My morning would be filled with people asking me questions about God, life, and religion. I felt I had a responsibility to my "sheep." After all, they couldn't see a shepherd who struggled, who doubted, who this very day was asking many of the same questions they had. So I had subtly created an image of who I wanted to be, or more accurately, of who *they* wanted me to be. Perpetuating the image of authenticity had become more important than being authentic.

Now don't get me wrong. I was sincere. At least, I sincerely wanted to be sincere. Actually, I sincerely wanted to be sincere about my sincerity. This whole faith and doubt thing was getting so complex. The pressure I had bought into, to be the paragon of faith and virtue to my tribe, had taken me down a path I didn't want to go. I was acting, filling a role, trying to be more than I was — and in so doing I had become less than what I was. I didn't want to live that way, and I was sure my faith community didn't want me to either. I knew they didn't. It was a commitment we had made from the beginning — "Be real people that know and worship the real Jesus."

Can you identify? Have you been busy pretending to believe? Keeping yourself looking good with spiritual activities — teaching Bible studies, going to prayer meetings, attending spiritual retreats, working in the homeless shelter—because you are afraid that once you stop doing, doubt will stalk you? If so, something in your spirit is likely whispering that just pretending won't support the weight of your *real* life.

Now don't go abandoning all those activities just yet. It may not be the activity that is the culprit, but you. You may be losing your true friendship with Jesus in the midst of acting like you have a better one than you do. In other words, pretending to be something you are not is making you less than what you actually are.

Jesus doesn't want to be our imaginary friend. He wants our faith in him to actually bear the weight of our lives. Getting there from here means being willing to turn off the television. We have to stop distracting ourselves and pretending to have more of a relationship with him than we do.

▸STOP, ▸LOOK, & LISTEN

1. Which aspects of your faith journey seem solid? Which ones seem to rest on a bit more shaky ground? What makes the difference (experience, intellectual understanding, and so on)?

2. Explore with some friends the difference between faith, obedience, trust, and pretending—especially what it means in your life. You may need to do this over latte or a whole pot of coffee, because it could take awhile.

Perhaps, like me, you have found that your spiritual journey hasn't been neat and organized, like a tidy little roadmap or GPS tracking device. If that's the case, you'll be encouraged to know you're in good company.

Find Comfort from Those
Who Have Doubted Before You

When I first read the newspaper article regarding one of my heroes of the faith, I was stunned, "[Her] exterior sunniness masked an astonishing secret—known to a handful of clergy counselors but no other close colleagues—that was revealed only through research for her sainthood candidacy."[2]

What was she hiding? Was I about to find out that another spiritual leader was embezzling funds or abusing parishioners? I mean, this is Mother Teresa I am talking about! How could she do anything wrong? Though I knew her only through books, articles, and an occasional Discovery Channel episode, I thought we were close. What could she have hidden so well from me?

I longed to emulate her closeness to Jesus and her ability to minister to the broken. What an encouragement to learn that we had more in common than I could have ever imagined. The article continued, "Mother Teresa was afflicted with feelings of abandonment by God from the very start of her work among the homeless children and dying persons in Calcutta's slums. From all available evidence, this experience persisted until her death five decades later. . . . "[3]

Holy sacred cows, Batman! The woman, whom I had made a saint in my heart, consistently struggled with doubt and abandonment issues, just as I have. What a relief! Indeed, Mother Teresa was a *real* person who knew and loved the *real* Jesus. Yet throughout her writing, she made mention of times when God felt distant and she felt the pain of loss of connection with God's love. But unlike those who are stuck in spiritual suburbia, she didn't try to distract herself from that pain. Instead, this godly woman allowed it to draw her closer to God. She said, "We cannot long for something that is not intimately close to us."[4]

So have countless saints of the historic Christian faith, including Saint John of the Cross. He coined the phrase "dark night of the soul," referring to those times when we can not understand what God is doing and feel distant from him.

What Saint John calls "dark," Luke the apostle calls a "gap." Dr. Luke emphasized the gaps that exist between God and us. In one story, he shares how God honors the person who recognizes the gap and shuns the person who doesn't (Luke@18:9-14). In another he tells of a centurion who kept a gap between himself and Jesus (Luke@7:7). Luke also tells how Jesus came for those who see the gap, but still trust in the Father's goodness (Luke@5:31-32). In other words, Luke affirms that there is a disparity between what I believe to be true and the actual reality I walk in. I am caught between two worlds — the kingdom reality that Jesus invites me to live from and the broken world the Enemy wants me to stay trapped in.

Mother Teresa, Saint John of the Cross, and Luke all expressed frustration: frustration with living in the tension of mystery but longing for the security of understanding. Frustration with believing in something they couldn't see, but also doubting that it even exists. They wondered if the labor of pursuing Christ would indeed reap the life-giving rewards he has promised.

One thing is clear, these saints also became aware that such disparity between where we live and what we long for can actually be a part of God's plan, part of his plan to set us free from suburbia and move us into his purposes. They realized that, although such seasons may not be comfortable, they are necessary. They solidify our faith and keep us from becoming hollow. We must be willing to walk in this gap.

Mother Theresa called the gap feeling abandoned, Saint John of the Cross called it "darkness," and yours truly, Saint Eric the Short One, calls is a necessary pain in the butt.

Yep, my life has been full of detours, roadblocks, and lurching starts. I often find myself wandering through neighborhoods I shouldn't be in, out of gas when I need to be making good time, and feeling flat when I should be all pumped up. But during those times, I don't just throw my faith away.

Instead, I stop and try to figure out where I am or what's causing the problem. Of course, being a guy, I have to be *very* lost before I ask for directions. Still, some of my greatest discoveries have occurred when I have felt the most spiritually lost or helpless. Perhaps that is because God likes to make sure we are at the end of our resources and wit before he steps in. That way we won't claim credit for the work he has done. So don't treat feeling lost like your enemy, because it may actually be your path to a deeper relationship with your friend. Let me show you what I mean.

▸STOP, ▸LOOK, & LISTEN

1. Go through the lives of some of your favorite Bible characters, watching for times when they struggled, doubted, or failed. What choices did they make during those times of struggle? What were the outcomes of those choices?

2. Next time you are in a period of doubt or discouragement, be honest with Jesus about it. Try being creative: write a poem or sing a song (it may sound like a country song), draw a picture, or talk out loud to the sky, hoping God is listening. Then wait for an answer.

My Faith Crisis

My team and I were ministering in the small river village of Porto de Moz, Brazil. We'd been there for a week. I had a good friend who was the pastor of a small church in this rural, impoverished community, which is only accessible by boat or plane. Our presence as American missionaries provided some great publicity for the final evening's church meeting. A hundred or so people packed the minuscule structure, and God was on the move. I preached what I thought was a powerful word for the community, and the air was charged with faith and encouragement.

I can't recall ever feeling so much in "the zone." People were coming to Christ and being filled with the Holy Spirit. I felt like a spiritual Shaquille O'Neal posting up against the Smurfs. The Enemy's defenses in this city and church were being shattered.

Then it happened. The mass of people up front parted like the Red Sea, to make way for a mother, sheepishly walking toward me, with her six-year-old boy tucked behind her. I could tell by the reaction of those around that this young woman was well-known. Through the translator, she simply said, "Please ask that God would heal my son." She showed me the boy, who was paralyzed down the entire left side of his body. Half his face drooped. His left arm and leg hung limp and lifeless.

As I knelt down to be eye-to-eye with this precious child, he moved to hide behind his mother's hip. His life had been six years of hell. In a land where survival was the goal and weakness a liability, he had been teased, beaten, and ridiculed. But a mother's love had brought him to a place of worship that night.

I reached out my hand and took hold of his good one. Immediately something began to surge through me like liquid love. It's hard to explain, but I loved this boy as my own. He felt it also, because he immediately stepped away from his mother and moved toward me. I looked into his hollow, but trusting eyes, and began to pray for his physical healing.

Oh, my faith was so high at that point. Still feeling the presence of God from the meeting, coupled with the love and compassion I had for this young man, I knew God would heal this boy. And so I prayed. . . . I could still feel the waves of liquid love flowing through me, but there was no physical manifestation of healing occurring in his body. My faith thermometer dipped just a bit.

While I prayed more holy words out loud, I found myself silently beginning to negotiate with my Lord Jesus. *Lord, all these people are here and experiencing your presence. What a statement it will make to this community when you heal this boy.*

Nothing . . .

Jesus, this is going to be a really bad PR move if this boy doesn't leave here healed. I know how much you love him, now please heal him.

Still nothing . . .

Negotiation was turning to begging, while I tried to keep up my very best faith-filled persona. *Jesus, I've done what you've asked me to do on this trip. I've left my family at home and spent all this time and money to be here. Please, at least for me, would you heal this child?*

I began to feel an unholy vacuum within.

Jesus, this is just not right. This mother comes to you as her only hope, and you are going to let her leave here shattered. It's just not right.

At that point, the negotiating ceased. I knew the healing wasn't going to happen, though I didn't know why. I stood up and let go of the little boy's hand. In my heart, all of the incredible things God had been doing that night were being crushed under the weight of my burgeoning disillusionment and embarrassment.

I gave my best cheesy pastoral smile to the mother and turned to walk away. I wanted to run and hide, but my heart made me turn and say one last thing to the mom. "Look, I don't know why God didn't heal your son. I wish I did. But I can tell you one thing: He loves your boy. I have never felt so much love and mercy flowing through me from God toward an individual as when I touched his hand. I'm sorry."

As I turned to leave, the mother burst into tears. "God loves my son! God loves my son!" she kept saying. As I found out later, when she had been eight months pregnant, her brother and another guy got into an argument and her brother was murdered right in front of her. The horror of that trauma sent her into premature labor. That crisis, coupled with poor medical procedures, seemed to have caused the paralysis her son has lived with ever since. She had thought God had abandoned them both. Perhaps more than healing of the body, they both needed healing of the heart and Jesus met them at that place. *Their* deeper questions had been answered—but *mine* were just beginning.

I decided to be transparent with my team and share with them my frustration. But, despite their counsel and prayer, I just couldn't stop the disillusionment from mushrooming within me. The twenty-eight hours of flights home only fertilized the fungus. I wanted so desperately to hear *why* from Jesus. I wanted to feel secure again in Father God's arms, knowing that even though the situation didn't work out the way I felt it should have, I was okay anyway.

Now, hold on to your theological safety nets. I knew in my head the proper church answers to such a dilemma. But the gap between what I knew in my head and what I felt in my heart was much wider than the physical eighteen inches. And God's silence on the matter was crushing me.

Upon our return, doubt tainted my sharing of stories with friends and family. Discouragement stalked me during times of study and solitude. When asked to pray for the sick, I stepped aside so "others could participate." I was dealing with a growing wave of disillusionment that was drowning my calling.

In our culture, we have been taught that disillusionment is a bad thing, but in reality it can be very healthy. After all, disillusionment helps us to understand that we have been living with an illusion. God wants us to walk in reality and life, not some beer commercial. He invites us to live life from his perspective, not from some politically correct, poll-driven, hyper-genderized, extremist center (whatever that is).

The easy road of pat answers and pretend certainty lulls us into a catatonic spiritual stupor. Some of the most boring Christians I know are ones who have every question answered, every behavior controlled, and every hardship glossed over with some pious Christian slogan. Spiritual suburbia has roads that are so smoothly paved and so straight and flat that if we looked west we could see the back of our heads.

Still, some well-meaning Christians offered me verses such as, "We know that in all things God works for the good of those who love him," and " 'For my thoughts are not your thoughts, neither are your ways my ways,' declares the LORD." Now I'm not saying the Bible is not true or helpful. In fact, when God finally did speak, these same verses suddenly found new substance for me. But the attitude in which these pat answers were given only proved my point. Cheez Whiz Bible answers spread thin on my experience in Brazil didn't cut it. I needed Jesus to talk to me—through his Word, through his ways, through my heart.

Then one day, I realized that maybe I would *never* hear from God about that situation, that I may never know why he didn't heal that child, and that God was asking me to choose to be okay with that. Even though I didn't understand why God hadn't answered our prayers for healing, I understood that I had to choose to trust him, and not allow discouragement to cause me to stop praying for the sick or caring for the broken.

How was I able to choose trust in the midst of doubt and disillusionment? I can't tell you this realization came through some amazing revelation off of TBN Channel 142. I can't tell you I received a Fed-Ex package from the Vatican containing a book entitled *Answers to Faith's Hardest Questions.* Restored faith came through wrestling with God in the silence. It came through re-evaluating many of my preconceived ideas regarding how God should work on my behalf. It came through remembering all the times on my journey when I had seen God act in me and through me. As a result, I was not willing to let the acid of disillusionment eat up my faith. God's love and forgiveness in my own life had just been too powerful and too redemptive to let something like this destroy my love for him.

So I chose to trust and let God's way be a mystery and not a misery in my life—and then God spoke. He let me in on the reasoning behind his little life lesson. "Eric, if you want the thrill of victory, you will have to learn to live with the agony of defeat. I am more concerned with your trust *in* me than I am your understanding *of* me."

▸STOP, ▸LOOK, & LISTEN

1. Has God ever let you down? Have you ever had a hope or dream shattered? Where are the pieces now?

2. How great is the distance between what you know about God's love and what you feel? Between what you know about God's power and what you experience? Between his forgiveness ... justice ... and so on? What can you do to close the gap?

Let God's Word — Not Your World — Determine Your Course

During my crisis of doubt, I had to decide whether I would stay obedient to what I once believed to be true. Would God's Word and not my world determine the course I would walk? Indeed there are times you and I must simply choose to follow God's Word, even when it doesn't feel right. To escape suburbia, we must take time and listen. Listen to God's Word. Listen to God's words. Listen to God.

That's the thing about the Bible; it transcends experiences much better than do my feelings or others' opinions. So during those times when fear, doubt, or disillusionment is calling us to safety and predictability, we must choose to take God at his Word:

- God says trust him — something we must do during times when our feelings would tell us to trust our human nature. (John@14:1)
- God says seek him — something we can only do when he is seemingly nowhere around. (Jeremiah@29:13)
- God says feed the poor, pray for the sick, set the

captives free — things that are not always glamorous or politically correct. (Isaiah@58:6-7)

I encourage people never to make a big decision when in a crisis. If we wait a little while, until the dust of circumstances settle and our emotions are a bit more stable, the path God wants us to take is usually clearer. Obedience and discipline do something for us. They give us rails to ride on, even when the way seems unclear.

Still, God has not created us to walk through these valleys alone. Healthy, life-giving relationships can add perspective and momentum out of the land of spiritual suburbia. Until then, honesty is the best policy.

Be Honest with God and Others

In order to keep from traveling superficially through life as great pretenders, we must be willing to be brutally honest and admit everything is not kosher in our souls. While the spirit of suburbia says insulate yourself and pretend everything is fine, we must choose to walk in the opposite spirit and pursue the God of our understanding. Sometimes God *hides* because he wants us to *seek*!

During my season of discouragement and doubt, I tried to remain faithful to what I was called to do. I tried to talk to God over and over again about it, even though his silence was sometimes deafening. Still, I knew there was a reason for the silence, and for the time being, that had to be enough. I had to choose to believe.

The great worshiper, David, also felt God's silence at times. The trusted friend of Jesus, Martha, struggled with his absence when her brother died. The faithful prophet John the Baptist even questioned Jesus' motives. Struggling with the "whys" and "where are yous" of faith puts us in good company. The common denominator in all those biblical saints is what should be common in us — they asked hard questions.

They pursued God. They were brutally honest with their struggle. They were not afraid to ask what was difficult. And sometimes they got a hard answer. Whether through singing a psalm of frustration on a hillside, through a personal confrontation, or through sending word from a prison cell, they took their struggle to the Master instead of throwing in the towel of faith. Ultimately, their doubt and discouragement provided great fertilizer for deeper trust and revelation.

To learn from doubt and discouragement, we must turn off the distracting gadgets spiritual suburbia so readily supplies to us. We must get up and listen *through* the silence *to* the voice of the Holy Spirit. There are numerous tools (spiritual disciplines) available to aid in that process. In his book *Celebration of Discipline*, Richard Foster explores these tools, and points out that tools are tools, not magical formulas or legalistic codes of conduct to earn God's favor. They exist to quiet our soul and invigorate our faith.[5] Here are a few spiritual disciples from Foster's book that help me move to a deeper place of confidence and understanding:

- **Simplicity:** Too much stuff cluttering your house, much less your mind? Too many things to clean, maintain, and pay for? Scale back. Could you live without it? Then try to. One way to do this is to identify things around you that have function versus fad. Functional things help us live, faddish things want us to live for them. My Native American friends have taught me the value of giving things away to bless others instead of holding on to things to bless myself. So attempt to downsize, not super-size your life.

- **Silence:** Having a hard time thinking clearly? Are thoughts getting jumbled? Refuse to turn on any noise-making device tonight (that may include your spouse). The regular exercise of silence can flush our minds clean of unwanted noise. It is not easy in today's culture, but that is why it is a discipline.

- **Fasting:** Okay, so there is nothing fast about it. But fasting can help us know if something owns us or we own it. It is not just about food anymore. Try a technology fast, or a television fast, or even a church meeting fast. The idea is to replace the space with seeking and listening.

As you make space for God through the various disciplines of your faith, you are provided with the time and energy to be honest with him. But having the opportunity and taking it are two very different things. Don't slip into the "I'm getting all holy" routine because you are practicing a discipline. That's when we start pretending to be something we are not and end up with less than we started with. Instead, practice a discipline because you are desperate for God and his life-giving presence in your life, *right here, right now.* Purpose to stay honest with God, and you will discover he begins to get honest with you.

It's not like he doesn't know about your frustrations already. But when you express them to him, your heart and mind stop trying to figure stuff out on their own. Too many questions and doubts live rent-free in our minds, taking up space that

Wisdom wants to fill.

When you create space to get honest with God, you may not get answers immediately, but you will get peace. You may not have understanding right away, but you will experience faith. You may not see circumstances change right away, but you will gain perspective. Besides, practicing such disciplines and showing such honesty puts you in the company of pretty amazing saints. For them, the story was not so much about where they began, but about the roads they followed, and where they finished.

Like me, you can take comfort in the reality that many tried-and-true men and women of God have been there before. Some saints, and some not so saintly. Look for the footprints left by Saint John of the Cross, Mother Teresa, David the shepherd king, even Jesus himself.

You may even see some tread marks left by a size 9 pair of Doc Martens. Those would be mine. But don't follow them because they haven't totally found their way out yet.

CHAPTER FIVE

A POWERFUL SUV

On Discovery and Learning

TAKE A MOMENT TO ponder a few of the SUV commercials you have seen. You know, the ones with the 4 x 4 climbing up an impossibly steep hill, or flying over logs and creek beds while pounding down on the suspension. The ones where a soccer mom detours around traffic by climbing over a mountain in order to pick up her kids, who are desperately waiting for her out in the rain.

Do you know anyone with a SUV who has actually pulled off such stunts? No, of course not. Underneath these ads, in microscopic print, flash the words: "Professional driver on a closed course. Do not try this at home."

But we're okay with that. For most of us who own SUVs, it's just enough to know we *could* do something like that if we needed to. While just knowing we could explore unpaved territory may be okay for literal suburbia, it's not okay for the landscape of our spiritual lives. We are called to actually *live* the adventure God equips us for. Still, most of us settle for something less. We have a lot of knowledge about God, but are sadly lacking in vibrant experiences with God.

In Need of Being Saved (Again)

Once every two years or so, I have an encounter with God that makes me feel "saved" all over again. It's not that I feel misplaced, like my son's jacket that goes from lost to found four or five times during a school year. But every once in awhile, I fall into a spiritual rut, and then find myself sinking in the quagmire of my own self-preservation.

I was feeling this way several years ago when I met Frank, and he helped me get unstuck. When Frank was through with me, I felt like I had been saved all over again. Frank and I met halfway across the world while I was part of a short-term mission team in Budapest, Hungary. The mission team and I were performing street dramas, preaching the gospel, and being all-around ethnocentric, upper-middle-class Americans. Still, God was at work, and lots of people were committing their lives to Christ and capitalism through us. We would stand in the middle of any number of crowded bus and tram terminals and, through a translator, talk about how God had saved us and could save any person who wanted saving.

I met Frank as I was wandering around a public square, taking in the sights and reminding God how lucky he was to have a young evangelist like me on his team. During my humble stroll, I noticed a weathered and aged man playing a violin that had only three strings. His knuckles where knobby, and his fingers appeared to be as beaten down as his violin. As I approached, he screeched a tune that sounded remarkably like two cats in heat. While playing, he looked at me longingly, hoping this fine young American man would toss a few coins into his violin case. I obliged and gave the man some coins.

Then I showed him the cool Jesus Movement replica

wooden cross I had hanging around my neck. Clasping my hands together, I pantomimed my question regarding whether I could pray for him. God loves the poor, and this man definitely fit that description. Perhaps a little encouragement from a man of God, such as me, would help him through another day. . . . But as I knelt down, the man extended one of his withered hands to my shoulder and raised the other one up to heaven, and began to pray for me instead. I don't speak Hungarian, so his words did not cast a spell on me, but something strange began to happen.

As soon as he touched me, I felt a tingling rush sweep over my body and then, *Wham!*, I hit the cement sidewalk, face first and weeping uncontrollably. Not the kind where you can simply dab a tissue to your eye, but the type where the snot valve opens and the tear faucet pours. I thought, *Get a grip, Eric. You are making a scene out here in public!* But my body would not submit to my pride. Instead, I lay there listening to an old man pray in a language I didn't understand, hoping no one was noticing me.

Okay, before you write me off as suffering from some version of jetlag psychosis, hear me out. I'll let you decide whether what happened next was actually a vision or a result of having just hit my head on the pavement, but this is the way I remember it. . . .

Another tingle went through me, and I found myself sitting at a colossal banquet table that stretched for hundreds of feet and seated hundreds of people. I was sitting on one end of the table, and Jesus was way, way down on the other side. I could hear him laughing and talking with those seated around him. Then I zoomed in on Jesus. Though we were still at opposite ends of this great expanse, Jesus and I were looking eye-to-eye—and he wasn't happy. "How many times have I told you that the first shall be last and the least shall be the greatest in my kingdom? You are kneeling before one of my most holy servants," he said.

Then like a hyperspace jump in *Star Wars,* I was back, face down on the sidewalk.

To this day, I don't know how long I was on the ground. It seemed like forever, but two American students told me they had been watching for about ten minutes. Yep, it just so happened that while God was opening a can of whoop on my pride, two Hungarian students who attended the American university had "stumbled" across the scene. "We see you've met Frank," they said.

"Uh, yeah, I guess so," I replied. "Can you tell me what he has been saying?"

"Well, he was praying. Frank was thanking God for sending such a holy man to his city so that many might receive God. He must think you're a priest or something. Then he went on to pray about the poor and needy around the city."

The only words I could muster were, "Trust me, I'm no saint."

The students went on to explain how Frank plays his violin every day in order to raise donations so that he can buy bread and distribute it to the poor and addicted who suffer without hope in the back alleys of Budapest. If Frank has any bread left-over after his rounds, then he'll eat. Rumor had it that there had been times when Frank had gone seven or eight days without eating so that others would have enough food.

And he thought I was holy. . . .

My encounter with Frank saved me from thinking that wearing a cool wooden cross around my neck made me a saint.

Talk about a spiritual rut! Yep, Eric, the self-labeled international evangelist, got saved that day. A holy man in Budapest led me to Christ. I know now that some of the poorest people in the world have the richest access to God's heart.

What a world of distance between my Christian suburbia and Frank's urban wilderness. Oh sure, I may have been able to dance doctrinal circles around him regarding God's heart for the poor and broken. I probably could have helped him set up a more effective and efficient way to collect money and distribute bread to the poor (all in the name of godly stewardship, of course!). But I wasn't the expert on ministry to the poor; Frank was.

Those of us who live in spiritual suburbia have become experts on what we don't experience. We attend our large group meetings, listen to other people talk about faith issues, and can critique sermons, services, and sanctity — *without ever having to interact with God ourselves.* The more and more we listen and observe as passive learners, the more we become experts of what we don't experience, but boy can we talk a good line.

▸STOP, ▸LOOK, & LISTEN

1. What is the difference for you when your faith is challenged and stretched versus when your spiritual life is in a rut or merely coasting?

2. Are you an expert about some things you haven't ever experienced in your faith journey? What are they? How might you take some steps toward experience in those areas?

Schmoozing with the Best of 'Em

Sometimes I can be such a schmoozer. I have this intense need to fit in and appear like I know what I'm talking about. Stick me in the middle of a group of guys talking about their 4 x 4 trucks, and I'll talk about lifters, mud tires, and gun racks with the best of them. Okay, so I don't hunt or own a gun; I mainly use my lifted Toyota 4Runner to drive over speed bumps and tailgate slow drivers. If I said someone had a nice rack in front of my wife, she would slap me—but that's the art of schmoozing. The guys I'm talking to don't have to know that. In fact, as long as they don't, I can sound like an expert on what I'm not experiencing.

Put me in the middle of some suburban renovators and I might even be able to convince them I know a lot about home redecorating. In reality, my wife has to threaten to throw away my Xbox just to get me to paint the living room, but I regularly watch *Trading Spaces* and *Extreme Makeover* on satellite television, and these shows have enabled me to sound like a professional decorator.

But you and I aren't called to be posers in the kingdom of God. Simply reading about or recycling other people's testimonies of God's miraculous intervention and faithfulness doesn't cut it. Sure, what God has done in and through other people can be used to propel our faith and motivate our wills, but sooner or later, each of us needs to get to doin' the stuff ourselves. Not stuffing ourselves with more information, more Bible studies, more pop-Christian entertainment. But doin' the stuff Jesus did. Loving the unlovely, feeding the poor, embracing those who are shunned by society, inviting people into the life that he offers regardless of their skin color, gender, race, or orientation. We need to live the adventure in our time and day, just as Jesus lived it in his time and day.

For some reason, we think that if we can just learn a little more about God, we will keep getting closer to him. Granted, that statement contains an element of truth, but in my real-time relationships, the best way to get closer to people is to get closer to them. I mean, if they are across the room, I can either study them from a distance, or get up and go sit next to them and participate in what they are doing.

Is there a better way to get to know someone than to follow that person around, doing the same activities, and asking questions along the way? Asking questions such as, "Why are we here?" "How did you decide on this route?" or "Can you teach me how?"

Perhaps, like me, you need to explore some unpaved roads so that you can start living the adventure that Jesus offers. Perhaps you need to be saved from the trap of knowledge without experience. Saved from the rut of spiritual boredom. Saved from a faith that makes you feel trapped instead of set free. If so, climb on into the Jeep and hit the unpaved, open roads. Don't worry about the dirt. You were made for it.

How Do You Connect with God?

In order to travel from my rural town on the Northwest tip of Washington, I have to travel across the waters of the Puget Sound on an automobile ferry. Ferries are great places to meet people. One time, I met this hippie brother carrying a gunny-sack backpack. Cool guy. He had been everywhere I ever wanted to go and then some—Europe, India, England, Canada, and even Graceland.

We had a lot in common. I had a really cool mullet and he had dreadlocks. We both loved a good cup of coffee in the morning and enjoyed meeting people, regardless of their race or creed. I wore a necklace with a cross and so did he.

Actually, he had about six necklaces adorning his neck-line. Not the MTV "get your bling on" type. They were just simple, almost unnoticeable ornaments. Yet they all carried a distinct theme. One of them was a cross. The others included a purplish-hued crystal, an Islamic crescent moon and star, and a Star of David or a pentagram-looking thing. He even wore this tiny little Buddha that had been made into a necklace by tightly wrapping the leather cord around the Buddha's neck. A bit ironic, I thought.

Then he asked me, "So how do you connect with God?"

What a great question: *How do you connect with God?*

How do we?

I want to actually have a conversation with God. I want to explore how wide and deep and profound this Creator of the universe is. I want to experience how safe, how merciful, how tender this Almighty God can be. I want to find him outside of the clean and tidy roads of systematic theology and inside the mysterious places beyond my understanding.

It must be possible, because religious history is full of saints who have done so. They have grabbed hold of something more real than just religious jargon as they talked to God.

Stop Eating the Menu

Jesus wants to be the master of our lives, and this puts us in the position of becoming his apprentices. The way to get closer to God is not to study about him, but to participate with him.

"Follow me" surely implied that Jesus was going somewhere.

Reading the Bible for knowledge alone is like going to a restaurant and eating the menu but not the meal. Now don't freak out on me. I'm not about to go all anti-Bible on you. I know and firmly believe that the best way to know where God is and what he is like is through his holy Word. However, the meal is in relationship with the person of Jesus Christ, not in simply reading about what he offers.

Many Christians are starving because all we have done is eat the menu. We dissect it, know the order of the books, recite many of the main ingredients (sin, repentance, prayer, and so on), and we even know how much certain behaviors cost or benefit us. But do we actually *experience* those truths? Do we actually live the adventure Jesus offers, or are we content to just read about others who do?

Take, for instance, prayer. Do we really pray the way Jesus prayed? Do we really connect with God when we pray? Jesus said:

> "This is how you should pray: 'Our Father in heaven, hallowed be your name, your kingdom come, your will be done on earth as it is in heaven.'" (Matthew@6:9-10)

You probably can't read this prayer without falling into a certain rhythm and tone. But what if Jesus was giving us more than a static prayer here? What if this prayer is only the menu and not the meal? Could it be that there is more behind the Lord's Prayer than just the words on the page?

Of course there is. And perhaps you're beyond just reciting this prayer, word for word. Maybe, like me, you've studied its format, realizing that it's really a model prayer. In order to help us in our conversations with God, Jesus was giving us some rails to ride on.

We understand that God's name is holy (hallowed) and that our lives are to be oriented around seeing his kingdom come and his will be done. We know we should forgive others and trust God for our daily provisions. We may have even graduated to understanding the difference between intercession and supplication, and thanksgiving and praise. But if this model prayer doesn't lead us to conversing with God on a regular basis, we are falling way short.

We want to be Christlike in how we connect with God, right?

How did Jesus pray? What was his goal for us? In Sunday school, I was taught that we are called Christians—which according to Mrs. Hampenstand meant "little Christs." I guess that means I should be able to have a conversation with God like Jesus did.

Whenever he prayed, Jesus used one word that I believe revolutionized how we are to pray. This word invites you and me into God's story—into living from the blueprint of plans he has for us. This word puts us in our place. It sets the created universe in order. It establishes the connection that God desires to have with us. It is the very first word in Jesus' model prayer—*Father.*

When Jesus spoke this word to his earliest disciples, it shot out like a lightning bolt. Nearly all commentators agree that when Jesus talked to his Father, he almost always used the Aramaic term *Abba. Abba* was a nursery term, and in today's vernacular it would be "Papa" or "Daddy." With this word, Jesus is inviting us to experience the Father's complete, safe, and radical tenderness toward us. Our conversations with God need to start with our understanding of God as our *Abba.*

So, what kind of conversations do you have with God—and what kind do you want to have? And, on the more profound flip side, what kind of conversations does God want to have with you? I doubt God has a hard time focusing on us, but why do we have such a difficult time focusing on him? Does he leave our conversations together feeling frustrated because he couldn't get a word in edgewise, or exhausted because we spent three-fourths of the time looking beyond him toward our own thoughts and desires?

Jesus gave us the most fundamental ingredient for a powerful prayer life, for a life-giving conversation with God: knowing God and approaching him as our *Abba*. If we don't get this, if we don't come to God as our *Abba* and let him function in that role, we will always come up short in regard to what he wants for us in prayer.

Perhaps all of this is not new information to you. Maybe you know that Jesus prayed to *Abba* and that the word means "Papa." But has this information changed the way you actually connect with God? Knowing and actually experiencing and trusting this information are very different things.

I've read a little Watchman Nee, Thomas Merton, Madame Guyon, and even sprinkled in some Rick Warren for flavor. Wow, these guys and gals seem to hear and converse with God at profound levels. I'm thankful that they share their disciplines with guys like me. Now I have all the information I need to really converse with my friend Jesus like I know I should. Of course, just knowing how and actually doing something can be a pretty big leap for a guy with short spiritual legs like mine.

Take, for example, my encounter with the mystic Madame Guyon. Here is an incredible woman of God whose story I struggle to relate to, but whose writings invite me to move from information to action. Born in 1648 in Montargis, France, she married at age sixteen a man twenty-three years older than she was (I told you I have a hard time relating to her life). Her married life and her extended family life were almost constant turmoil.[1] She was forced to marry at sixteen, though she wanted to be a nun. After a horrid marriage and the loss of two children, she found herself a widow with three children at age twenty-eight. Her beginnings were depressing, oppressing, and life-stealing. Perhaps that's what drove her *into* the arms of God instead of away from him.

I first ran into Madame Guyon while studying Richard Foster's *Devotional Classics*.[2] She wrote about a profoundly simple way to turn our hearts toward the presence of God.

- First, find a Scripture to use to help you focus on God.
- Second, continue to read those words over and over again, *slowly*, until you sense God's presence.
- Third, shift from the Scripture to conversing with the Lord.
- Finally, if your mind wanders, just go back to the Scripture and use it to get you back on track.[3]

Good stuff, so I decided to do a little more research on this mystical woman. My research technique was "new school." I Googled her name and got more information than my mental CPU could handle. I discovered that Madame Guyon developed other cool ways to have conversations with the Creator—like how to pray the Scriptures and mediate for long periods of time.

I really learned a lot from her. Hmmm . . . that was about two months ago. Since then, I've gotten pretty good at talking about prayer. I might even preach a sermon someday, using Madame Guyon as a great example of faith and walking through the tough times in our lives. Yep, it has been a couple months now since God invited me, via Madame Guyon, to use Scripture to find his presence and thus override my normal ADHD-type distractions.

I know God is still waiting. . . . But there are still so many websites out there with other techniques and ideas to help me get closer to God. I'm sure I'll choose one soon.

Moving from the Menu to the Meal

Then there was Julian of Norwich. She wasn't content with just believing in the menu. She wanted all God had for her, even though life tried to give her something else. A mystic, she lived from 1343 to1413 as a Benedictine nun in Norwich, England. (It took me awhile, but I figured out that's how she got her name.) Her writings always pointed to the goodness and love of God, even though she was living in a time of severe social unrest and constant fear of the Black Plague.

This woman knew about connecting with God. She talked with him often. Here is what she said about prayer:

For the highest form of prayer is to the goodness of God . . . God only desires that our soul cling to him with all its strength, in particular that it clings to his goodness. For of all the things our minds can think about God, it is thinking about his goodness that pleases him most and brings the most profit to our soul. For we are so preciously loved by God that we cannot even comprehend it. No created being can ever know how much and how sweetly and tenderly God loves them.[4]

Can you sense how far out of suburbia Julian is inviting us to travel? *Clinging to God's goodness with all of my strength.* Geez, I hardly even know what that means, let alone how to practice it. But my spirit resonates with its truth. Like the sound of a native drum that I cannot see but feel drawn to find, God's goodness draws me closer. As I explore and cling to his goodness, I realize it is so massive I cannot comprehend it. I could drink from God's goodness and love all my days, and his well would never run dry, and my thirst would never be quenched. The invitation goes beyond understanding to truly clinging to the tangible nature of God's goodness.

But getting that close to God makes some people uncomfortable. I can hear the voices now. . . .

- *Wait . . . you don't know me. . . . I'm too messed up. I talk to God, but God wouldn't want to talk to me.*
- *Having that kind of intimacy with God is for super-Christians. My life is stale, and my sin often outweighs my success.*
- *I can't even focus on my checkbook; how am I supposed to tune into God?*

If such words have flowed from your thoughts, then listen to what Brother Lawrence, who is regarded as one of the closest men to God who ever lived, wrote:

I imagine myself as the most wretched of all, full of sores and sins, and one who has committed all sorts of crimes against his king. Feeling a deep sorrow, I confess to him all of my sins, I ask his forgiveness, and I abandon myself into his hands so that he may do with me what he pleases.

This king, full of mercy and goodness, very far from chastening me, embraces me with love, invites me to feast at his table, serves me with his own hands, and gives me the key to his treasures. He converses with me, and takes delight in me, and treats me as if I were his favorite. This is how I imagine myself from time to time in his holy presence.[5]

There it is again: someone who actually experienced the reality of connecting with God and didn't just talk about it. In his letters, Brother Lawrence told his disciple about the process he took in order to get out of suburbia and into the presence of God. He used his God-given imagination to enter into God's presence. He was not referring to some pop psychology or incantation. He used his imagination to clear space in his mind, soul, and spirit in order to receive everything God had for him. Not because he deserved it, but because he had learned God's love is unrestricted and immeasurable.

We can learn to do the same by refusing to become an expert on what we don't experience. So don't just study the radical tenderness that God has for you—ask *Abba* to be able to experience it. Don't settle for the stable, unemotional father figure that most churches infer God is. Sure, this kind of relationship with God seems safer and more predictable, but it is not what Jesus wants for you and me. Let God pour his *emotional, reckless, and prodigal* love on you.

I'm so thankful for my concrete face plant with Frank. He changed me by inspiring me. He changed me by helping me realize that authenticity is more than just the right look. He helped me understand that a conversation with God comes from a deeper wellspring than just my intellect. He taught me that spiritual power comes from a source far greater than a wooden icon around my neck. Thanks, Frank, wherever you are.

Not only do we tend to know more than we experience when it comes to prayer, we also do the same with our scholarship. In spiritual suburbia, we only read what reinforces what we already know. In the life Jesus offers, he wants us to take what's in our heads and use it to energize our feet.

▸STOP, ▸LOOK, & LISTEN

1. Go through Jesus' model prayer, using the idea of Papa God as the anchor. How does this reality influence the other parts of the prayer?

2. Maybe you'll get to Madame Guyon's meditation tool before I will. Choose a verse that communicates the goodness of God. Need help? Try Romans 8:38-39. Follow Madame's steps outlined earlier in the chapter.

Refuse to See Life Through the Yellow Lens

When I hit the ripe old age of thirty-one, I passed a major milestone in my life. There I was, nearly halfway to retirement, and I had just finished school. Thirteen years of public schools plus a decade of higher education had added up to a PhD (Debt Piled High and Deep). I'm sure I learned a lot during those years, but one thing I learned for sure was how to use a yellow highlighter.

Higher education teaches a person many valuable things, but none more than how to use a highlighter. The beauty of a highlighter is that it helps us set apart the points we've read or scanned that we feel are likely to be relevant come testing time. Later, instead of re-reading an entire textbook, we can just review the "highlights."

I used to think it was to my advantage to buy used textbooks that already had lots of highlights. But that was frustrating because previous colleagues didn't seem to know which things I would think were important. So I would just end up confusing their highlights with mine.

I get a kick out of the color-coordinated highlighter people. I see them at school and at church. They have four or five colors—the hot pink highlighter for vocabulary words, yellow for theory, green for research methods, and blue for names to know. I wish I were that color-coordinated. They shift through colors as they read and mark quicker than other students can find the selected passage in the text.

You can tell books that I really like by the amount of yellow when you flip through the pages. I have a small library of books, maybe a hundred or so. I've always wondered what would happen if I could just condense all the yellow into its own book and read the highlights of my own life's academic and spiritual journey.

A couple times a year, I go back through my selection of books and read the highlights. The bummer is how convicting that process is, because I see so many great points and insights that I wanted to apply to my life. Some I have, but most remain yellow. Of course, I find solace in the knowledge that I will apply them—someday. And if I ever need to be an expert on a topic, I won't have to read a bunch of new stuff. I can just scan a book and maintain the appearance of being the expert on what I'm not experiencing.

There is another interesting phenomenon regarding the books in my library. Most of the highlighting occurs in the front half of the books, with the amount slowly drying to a trickle by the three-quarter mark. Could it be that authors really only have good stuff to say in the front portion of their manuscripts, and that the rest is just dribble?

I don't think so. The real problem is me. I have a bad habit of not finishing books. I usually make it three-quarters of the way through before I get distracted with the next best book on my shelf. I do that a lot with my life. I love to start things, but finishing them often becomes a burden.

My friend Pat the Procrastinator was listening to Dr. Phil (or Dr. Laura or Dr. Ruth) the other day. Pat didn't finish listening to the program, but one thing he heard was that people would feel a lot better about themselves if they would just look at their lives and make an effort to finish what they started before moving on to something else.

Sounded good to him. So he finished off the bag of Cheetos he was eating and then went into the kitchen. He decided to finish the bottle of Merlot he and his wife had opened the night before. By this point he was feeling pretty good. So he concluded his self-esteem binge by spending the next four hours completing all the Halo 2 levels he had yet to conquer on Xbox and downed the rest of a bottle of Ritalin. By that point, he was feeling pretty freaky fine indeed. I'm not sure Pat understood what the good doctor meant.

I think I get it though. I've realized I need to apply what I have been learning. I need to follow through on the commitments I have made, especially the things that Jesus has brought into my life. Jesus may have been speaking to me through those books, but have the words worked their way into my being?

Let's not be content with a life of head knowledge that doesn't change our behavior. Listen to what Peter says: "His divine power has given us everything we need for life and godliness" (2 Peter@1:3). God wants us to escape suburbia by tapping into his power and presence in our lives and using it for life.

Turning Knowledge into Experience

Escaping spiritual suburbia means aligning our behaviors with our beliefs. In order to do that, we have to tap into God's power, which enables us to do what we're called to do and be who we're called to be. For me, that means trying to be a better husband. One who actually honors my wife and sees her as a gift. It means learning to hear her voice and to understand her deeper needs. Yep, that will take God's divine power. . . .

Applying the knowledge I already have means actually being a loving father who raises his kids in a way that helps them to own a deeper sense of values than what satellite television is teaching them. Yep, I need divine power. . . .

My beliefs tell me to keep my eyes pure, my tongue life-giving, my body healthy, and my friendships authentic and not manipulative (and to be able to discern between the two). Yep, I need divine power to be able to do that.

What an incredible idea. God has made his divine resources available to help us actually live. Not to just be hyper-religious, namby-pamby posers with about as much substance as a bowl of Cocoa Puffs. Instead, he wants his presence to be our "bread of life"—the sustenance that we need.

The divine power he offers is called grace. Yep, grace. Not the kind we say at the table before dinner when mom is around. Grace is something much more meaningful, tangible, and powerful. Grace is more than a doctrinal concept or theological presupposition. Grace is God's empowering presence in our life. It is what he gives us in order to help us turn knowledge into experience. Grace is what made the difference in Jesus' life on earth and Peter's life in the book of Acts. It's what can make the difference in our lives today. Check out these examples of the active difference made by the presence of God's grace:

- "And the child grew and became strong; he was filled with wisdom, and the grace of God was upon him" (Luke@2:40). If grace were only God's "unmerited favor" as some evangelicals have taught, would Jesus have needed it? No. What Jesus needed was the powerful presence of the Holy Spirit in his life to help him accomplish the task that was set before him. Grace in Jesus' life was active and tangible.
- "But by the grace of God I am what I am, and his grace to me was not without effect. No, I worked harder than all of them — yet not I, but the grace of God that was with me" (1Corinthians@15:10). Paul understood that God's grace was active and powerful. He was able to work harder, grow deeper, and have greater effect because of God's grace working in him.
- "For it is by grace you have been saved, through faith — and this not from yourselves, it is the gift of God — not by works, so that no one can boast. For we are God's workmanship, created in Christ Jesus to do good works, which God prepared in advance for us to do" (Ephesians@2:8-10). If grace were just a theological presupposition, how could it propel us to live the life Jesus has for us? God's grace saves us in the

present and continues to keep our hearts and bodies in line with his will as time passes — *if* we allow it to work in our lives.

To be able to take head knowledge and walk it out in the real world, we need grace. We need to begin to pray and ask God to take whatever sections we have highlighted in yellow in this book or that book or the Bible, and to empower our lives with that truth.

God, please make this a reality in my life. God, take what I have read and turn it into truth in my day. Don't let this one escape me, but work it out in me and through me!

I believe prayers like this don't go unheeded by God. When we open ourselves up to his empowering presence, it is like getting under the spout where the power comes out. Expect to see things changing inside you, not by your own effort or will, but by his grace. Because, after all, it is by grace you are saved, not by works. You don't get grace by earning it, and you don't keep it by controlling it. You get more grace by living it. The more of God's grace you allow into and through your day, the more he will pour upon you.

We aren't endued with such power and equipment merely to attend church by-law meetings or drive over the speed bumps of some stale church members' opinions regarding carpet color in the sanctuary. God has equipped us to charge over the gates of hell, to drive straight into the Enemy's camp, and to live a life that finds itself right smack in the middle of God's story in the world around us. Step on the gas, I see a mountain to climb. . . .

I hope you've highlighted some stuff in this chapter. . . . If what I write is God's grace through me, then what you will walk is God's grace through you. Leaving suburbia takes grace, and lots of it.

▸STOP, ▸LOOK, & LISTEN

1. Grab the last three books you have highlighted or been especially impressed with (even your Bible). Go back through and see if the points that grabbed you have actually changed you. Why or why not?

2. List five things about God or faith that you know a lot about but haven't really experienced. Are you content being an expert on what you don't experience? If not, how can God's grace help you to change?

CHAPTER SIX

A REALLY BIG HOUSE

On Intimacy with God

THE PEOPLE WHO WORK in the lost luggage department of airports have a lot in common with those who work with outhouses. Both think their job stinks, and both spend most of their days taking crap from other people.

I was reminded of this the other day while I waited twenty minutes in line in the bowels of the Seattle-Tacoma airport outside the lost luggage door. Resentment melted into life-giving grace as I listened to the professional man in front of me railing on the young clerk because the airlines had lost his precious suitcase, probably full of Tommy Hilfiger boxer shorts.

When it came my turn to make my lost luggage plea, the first words out of my mouth were, "I'm sorry you got treated that way. I'll try to be nicer."

Mr. Luggage Guy replied, "Oh, he's probably in a hurry to get into his great big car, drive to his great big house, and turn on his great big television so he can ignore the great big emptiness he feels toward his great big wife."

Dude, you've got to get out of this basement more.

Perhaps it is the psychology major in me, but Mr. Luggage Guy's comments got me thinking a lot about the types of homes people return to. Not just the physical structures, mind you, but the relationships behind the brick and mortar walls.

Drive around the suburbs of any major metropolitan city, and you'll find street after street of cookie-cutter homes. Sure, some of the landscaping changes, but from the rooflines to the garage doors, things look pretty much the same. Now, there is nothing wrong with the affordability that suburban living offers on the outside. But what happens on the inside of these homes? The people they contain can have lives full of intimacy or lives of discord.

The difference is determined by where they are expending their energies—keeping up an exterior façade or keeping up the relationships within those walls? When you live in a large home, you have plenty of room for a variety of activities to be happening at once, but it also means you don't have to be very close to anyone if you choose not to be.

This book is about the home located inside of you. It is about the space within your soul. There is so much territory, there are so many rooms, within our souls that God wants to explore. There are so many ways we could get to know him, if we would only take the time to open the door and invite him in.

Jesus said in Revelation 3:20, "Here I am! I stand at the door and knock. If anyone hears my voice and opens the door, I will come in and eat with him, and he with me." As Jesus spoke these words he was talking to the church. Those who already professed to have relationship with him. So why would he be asking to come in? Maybe he was tired of living in the spiritual suburbia of the church.

A shared meal to a Jew was a deep sign of intimacy and care. People didn't share meals with ESPN playing in the background or within twenty minutes so they could hurry off to the next event. Mealtime was an investment of time, trust, and intimacy. Jesus wants to be invited into deeper, more meaningful relationship than just standing at the door will allow.

Yet, that's about as intimate as we often get with him.

Cosmic Pizza Man

I have a relationship with my pizza guy, but it looks nothing like the relationship I have with my kids or my wife. When the pizza man comes to the door with my double pepperoni, double cheese, thin-crust special, I don't grab hold of him, tickle his ribs and wrestle with him on the floor, as I do with my kids. Nor do I kiss him passionately, nibble on his ear, and ask if we're going to get lucky later, as I often do with my wife.

Nope, instead I give him a courteous thank you, some cash with a 12.5 percent tip, and take from him what I asked to be delivered. Then I slam the door, turn my back on him, and go munch some grub.

The ludicrous notion of tickling my pizza guy got me thinking about the relationship many of us have with God. Many of us only see God as a cosmic pizzaman. We hold him at arm's length and limit just how close he can get to us in order not to feel uncomfortable. We perceive that his only job is to deliver to us what we are asking, and to do so in thirty days or less. God is there, all right, waiting and hoping that we will call so he can serve us. We take advantage of his service when we need it, and if he does a good job, we may even tip him 10 percent.

We are so accustomed to suburbia's consumer-driven, me-first orientation that we carry that same attitude over to our faith. We are more passionate about consumerism than we are about missions. I see this in my own prayers.

God, I need you to get me this. . . .

God, our toilet is broken, please provide funds for another.

God, if you'll help this lottery ticket win, I'll give 10 percent to the church . . . okay and another five percent to missions.

God, please help my kids respect me more. Oh, while you're at it perhaps you could give a dose of that respect stuff to my wife as well. . . .

When we view God as our cosmic pizza guy, we know what to expect of him: give me, give me, give me. We sound like we're the lord of the "Me's" Preschool. Secretly we hope that our plastic Jesus' head is bobbing up and down, saying yes and not wagging back and forth, saying no.

Now don't get me wrong. I know God cares about us and is Jehovah Jirah (the Lord who provides). But JJ is not the label on his butler jacket or the mission of his heavenly host. God desires an intimate relationship with us—his creation. Our purpose, ultimately, is to love and serve and bring honor to him. We may know that theologically, but do we demonstrate it experientially? When he invites us to go further in our relationship with him, does it feel as awkward as the idea of greeting the pizza guy with a long and passionate kiss?

We should never allow barriers to grow between God and us. He wants to pull us past what we see as comfortable and safe and have us explore deeper and more meaningful areas of intimacy with him than we ever thought possible. But that means getting away from routines that merely keep God as a part of our weekly schedule and not a part of our everyday lives. It means taking some risks to love and trust him in ways we haven't experienced before.

▸STOP, ▸LOOK, & LISTEN

1. Take some time and ask yourself, "Could I be experiencing more with God or is this it?" Look beyond the horizon of what you know to what you long to know. What do you see?

2. Draw a picture of a great big house that represents your life. The rooms and closets represent various aspects of your life. Are there some rooms Jesus isn't welcome in? Are there some closets that are hidden?

As Jesus pulls us forward into deeper communion with him, we pass through another level of intimacy with God — the business relationship.

The Business Partner

Life in spiritual suburbia often convinces us that life with God is as good as it gets when we develop a great working relationship with him:

- We know God by name and commit to working for him because we believe in the vision and values of his organization.
- We spend a lot of quantity time with him discussing how to meet the various needs of the organization.
- We hold finance meetings with him in order to plan building campaigns, raise money for the poor, and work out strategies to get other members contributing part of their paychecks to the organization.
- We even hold marathon PR meetings passionately developing plans to sell his product (salvation) to others.

It becomes a relatively stable symbiotic relationship—one where we mutually benefit each other. Because of this, many of us allow our relationship with God to plateau here, in the land of suburban symbiosis. After all, we have a great working relationship with our Master. We get his peace and fire insurance, and he gets our busy bodies. We get lots of potlucks and social networking opportunities, and he gets our tithe.

The temptation to settle in this land is powerful. It is, after all, the Land of Good Things:

- It is good to focus on evangelism and reaching the wanderer.
- It is good to serve others on Sunday mornings. Whether in Sunday school, as part of the worship team, by preaching, or greeting guests.
- It is good to commit to social justice issues and bring God's love to the broken.
- It is good to lend support to committees and Bible study groups.

But in the midst of all these good things, we can forget to stop and ask why. Why am I so busy? From what core does all this effort stem? Am I fulfilling the Great Commission merely because I'm supposed to, or because of the accolades, or because my heart is burning with love for the people God misses?

I know far too many pastors and Sunday school teachers that teeter around the edge of burnout, simply because they are no longer satisfied with middle management in the kingdom of God. They signed up because they loved the Boss and grooved with his vision. The benefits were out of this world and the coworkers were friendly. Then something began to happen.

Their external busyness dried up the internal goodness they once possessed. Once motivated by the Master himself, they are now only motivated by the machine itself; they are simply a cog in the wheel of the business called "churchianity."

That's what happened to my friend Jonathan. His conversion to Christ was radical and life-changing. Born and raised in East Los Angeles, he grew up street smart and tough. When Jonathan was twenty, God grabbed hold of his heart, held it in his nail-pierced hands, and turned this six-foot-four, three-hundred-pound, Hispanic, Hollywood punker into a gentle giant for Jesus.

Early in his walk with God, Jonathan's passion often outweighed his wisdom. He invented the ministry of "evandelism." He combined vandalism with evangelism by spray-painting cars or New Age store windows with messages such as "Jesus loves you." On other occasions, he would flatten the tires of parked cars and wait for the owner to return. Then, like an angel in waiting, he would approach the owner and offer to fix their flat for free if they would listen to his message of God's love.

Jonathan's methods never took the evangelical church by storm, but his worship did. He was a gifted and passionate musician. His love for Jesus found its way through the chords he played on his guitar and the songs he sang to his Savior. He soon found himself playing for crowds and leading church worship teams. People gathered around *his* fire and warmed up in *his* glowing.

Jonathan liked what he saw in the response of others. His pastor liked it too, and a subtle shift began to happen within Jonathan's heart. He started playing for the effect of worship. He slowly lost his personal fire and was no longer playing to an audience of One. It became his profession to lead others into the presence of God and "warm them up" for the pastor's message. Slowly, subtly, and surely, this once radical, passionate, no-holds barred, worshipper of Jesus had turned his ministry into a business relationship.

Before he knew what had happened, the goal of Jonathan's music was to create and perpetuate the sense of God's presence for others on Sunday mornings — even though that presence had long since waned in his own heart. He had convinced himself that it was good to be a team player and serve the church, even though he was beginning to feel a bit hollow. His songwriting came to a halt, and the music in his heart started to fade.

Jonathan found himself becoming bitter toward his pastor and resentful of church meetings. As he took time to look around his life and ministry, he realized that this wasn't what he had signed up for. Jonathan's revelation came when he realized that his worshipping heart had lost its center. Everything felt shallow. What he'd once done for the love of Jesus, he was now doing for the works of Jesus. He was doing good things, no doubt, but somehow it wasn't flowing from the same passionate core.

So Jonathan stepped outside of the worship suburbia he had created and went looking for the fire that had once burned in his heart. He found it by taking time to love Jesus in private, honor his wife more than ministry, and find a church that valued his character more than his gifts. Today, Jonathan's worship burns brighter than ever.

It is so easy for us to drift toward simply acting as if we are intimate with Christ, when the truth is that we are simply functioning out of a sense of duty, just as we might with a business partner. We chant the mantra of the organization and enjoy the sense of security we feel when we see our commander-in-chief pictured on the wall.

But down deep, do you ever wonder if God would really love you even if your job performance weren't up to snuff?

Do you wonder if God would just enjoy your company and not just your activity?

If so, know that there is a way out of spiritual suburbia. But it means taking a risk. It means pushing some boundaries and getting out of your routine. It means believing in, hoping for, and pursuing the intimacy that lies beyond the borders of the working-class Christian life, starting with experiencing God as your friend.

▸STOP, & LISTEN
▸LOOK,

1. This is a painful section for many of us to read because we have been chewed up and spit out of the organization of the church (like Jonathan), or because we recognize the gnawing on our souls. Don't be too quick to blame the system. Ask God what your part has been in the process that brought your heart from fullness to emptiness.

2. Remember, Jesus really loves his church, although he often grieves over its actions. Are you willing to extend forgiveness and healing to the body of Christ?

The Good Friend

My team and I were working among the children who were living and working in the desolate and polluted environment of a garbage dump on Bohol Island in the Philippines. Smoke from the piles of burning debris filled the air, burning my lungs and eyes. Hundreds of thousands of flies hovered just over the ground, feasting on the remnants of a nearby city's life.

A friend Marty and I had just returned from walking around the area, inviting children to our base of operations for some lunch and medical attention. The team was administering first aid to a boy with second and third-degree burns all over his feet. He said that, three days before, he had been walking barefoot in the garbage, salvaging things to sell or eat, when he slipped through some charred crust into a fissure of red-hot, smoldering coals. He had fashioned some makeshift flip-flops out of string in order keep working. We medicated his feet, wrapped them with gauze, gave him some shoes, and prayed God's love all over him.

There I was, doing the "business" of the church: offering mercy and healing to the poor and broken. But I had a secret agenda on this excursion. I truly longed to learn what it meant to build a cooperative friendship with Jesus. From the beginning of the trip, I committed to spending an hour with God *before* any work was done. Sometimes that meant getting up as early as 5 a.m. (with no Starbucks around!). Before I got busy doing the work of the church, I wanted to know the leader of the church.

Jesus tried to communicate to his followers that there was a difference between friends and business partners (servants). While on the outside the work might look the same, the relationship between friends who work together and business partners who work together is very different. Jesus told his followers, "You are my friends if you do what I command. I no longer call you servants, because a servant does not know his master's business. Instead, I have called you friends, for everything that I learned from my Father I have made known to you" (John@15:14-15).

The difference between being a servant and a friend is in the intimacy, not the action. We are called to do the things that Jesus did—feed the poor, heal the sick, care for the broken and widows, love his church, and serve one another. We can be religious and do these things out of a sense of duty, or we can be intimate and do them out of a sense of friendship. I, for one, want to be in a cooperative friendship with Jesus, where he shares with me not only the task at hand, but his heart's desires and motivations as well.

Developing a cooperative friendship with Jesus was something new for me. I knew that the relationship I had with Marty was the kind of relationship I longed to have with Jesus. Marty and I could wrestle through the emotional and spiritual impact of our journey together while we were doing the work we felt called to do. God used my relationship with Marty to invite me to a deeper one with Jesus.

I knew that if I wanted a friendship with Jesus, I had to do more than simply invite him over to my house to play Xbox and Life. If I wanted to be his close friend, I would need to go and do the things he enjoyed, things such as caring for the poor and loving the broken, and that I needed to do those activities out of a deeper and more transparent relationship with my Master. The problem is that I had done those things before and been successful, but as God's business partner. And success in the past often becomes a barrier to new growth in the present. Now I desired something deeper—a friendship with Jesus. While working with the outcast and feeding the poor were "good" things to do, they seemed more in the realm of *business* with God and not *friendship* with God. How could I bridge this gap? I found the answer came, not in action, but in more conversation.

My team had gathered about twenty children and had given them sandwiches and something to drink. The putrid fumes of burning trash wafted through the air, and our unaccustomed eyes were burning. One of the local worship leaders brought a guitar, and everyone was singing a song with words that translated to: "The Lord is gracious and compassionate. Slow to anger and rich in love. . . . He has compassion on those he has made. . . ." I knew the song well, but suddenly found myself feeling cynical.

Under my breath I muttered, "God, this song just isn't right. Look at the deprivation and pain these kids live in. How can we be singing that you are gracious and have compassion on those you have made?"

Then, suddenly, a wish I had made but never expected to come true materialized. It was as if Wisdom was standing next to me, for I heard a voice as clearly as if I were talking to my friend Marty, saying, "I sent you didn't I?" Those life-giving words, which I knew were from God, started a conversation with him like I had seldom had before. The kind where you are comfortable and safe, like sitting in your living room eating nachos and confiding in a friend.

It's hard to explain, but I felt as if God was saying that he was allowing me to be a part of his heart and love for these kids and the Philippines. He was not content to just have these kids cast aside by humanity. He loved them and cared enough to ask people from across the world to spend their own money to come prove it. Nothing was going to stand in the way of his reaching these kids—not economic status, national politics, or people's personal finances.

For the first time in my twenty-year Christian life, I was participating in a cooperative *friendship* with Jesus, not just a partnership. I was actually doing the work of the kingdom, but Jesus wasn't just calling me his servant, but also his friend. And as such it seemed he felt open enough to share with me his heart for those kids and for me.

Now, before you write me off as simply breathing in too much toxic air that day, ask yourself if what I'm describing is possible. Many of us are lured into being busy for God, while subtly sacrificing true relationship with him, the one we profess to love. But conversations like this one can turn something hollow to something hallowed. So slow down and listen to Jesus your master *and friend.*

If the Enemy can't take you and me out of the game, he would sure like to keep us so busy with life and church that we forget to pursue love and relationship with God. Like my relationship with Marty, my connection with Jesus tends to vacillate back and forth between work and friendship, but I know—indeed I have experienced—how good it can be. So today I purpose to do those things that Jesus is doing, *and* to ask him, "Can I cooperate with you as your friend, and not just as your business partner?"

Of course, friendship with God feels a lot safer for many than fatherhood. How far out of suburbia are you willing to drive?

▸STOP, ▸LOOK, & LISTEN

Ponder some of the "good" things you are doing for God. Is it possible to keep doing them, but from a deeper level of relationship? Could serving in your kid's school or being on the finance committee at church be done in cooperative friendship with Jesus and not just out of social or spiritual duty?

The Father Who Loves

Tonight my seven-year-old son showed me a wonderful picture he drew with a hybrid assortment of crayons, felt-tip markers, and a pencil. The crisp, white paper was drowned out by a flurry of red, flaming arrows, a hideous dragon with bulging eyes (that at first I thought was a cow on crack), and a couple of stick figures holding what looked like a birthday cake with too many candles. He anxiously told me that it was a picture of the two of us throwing a bomb and shooting arrows at a cow . . . uh, I mean Satan, the dragon. We were doing battle together, father and son, for God's sake.

"I made it for you, Daddy. Put it in your office," he said, with a proud-as-Picasso smile.

My first thought was that displaying this in my office would be a sure-fire invitation for a mental health evaluation of my son and the father who promotes such violence in small children. So I did what every loving father in America does with the art his children produce—I put it on the refrigerator. That way, every time I gulp some juice or grab a frozen Twinkie, I would be reminded, in a warrior-sort-of-way, I'm my kid's hero.

Just as I don't critique the art my children make for me,

neither does God critique our heartfelt worship works for him. Our church sanctuary is set up with three easel boards, professional drawing paper, and a tray of colored chalk and pencils. At various times during Sunday morning worship, someone draws a picture while simultaneously singing with the rest of the congregation. Sometimes the pictures these experimental worshippers create could be considered professional, other times they are . . . well . . . sincere, but hard to interpret. Regardless of the skill of the artist, the result is always the same. We post the productions on a section of the wall in our sanctuary. To us, the art is a way of saying, "I love you, Father God. Here is something to put on *your* refrigerator."

God wants us to draw near to him and trust him. He is a Father like no other. He rejoices in our accomplishments, holds us in our brokenness, and empowers us in our inadequacies.

But drawing near to God and trusting him as a Father is an unconquerable quandary for many.

This was brought home to me a few years ago when I was ministering with a group of Christian college students at a major university. God's goodness and power were evident as he fanned the flame of his gifts and callings in the lives of hundreds of individuals. Kris, my prayer partner, and I were praying for a young woman who said she wanted to know and experience the truth she had been told: Jesus loves you.

Sweet and easy, I thought. I believe God's love is as tangible as it is theological.

Enthusiastically, I placed my hand on her shoulder and began to pray, *Father God, pour your love upon this young woman. May she know and experience your Father's love in a profound way tonight.*

"Stop that!" this young student cried, as she pulled away.

"If you knew what my father did every time he said he wanted to love on me, you would never pray something so cruel. . . ." With that, she burst into tears.

Whoa. I had never encountered a real-life person whose perception of God had been so poisoned. I grew up in a home where a father's love meant attending my football games, helping me with math, and, as situations warranted, giving me a healthy swat on the butt or a gentle hug around the neck. Dad was there when I needed him. My father's love gave me life — he didn't steal it.

Like this young woman, many of us have a chasm between our theology and our experience. We have been taught that God is loving, but we've never experienced his love and we have trouble trusting it. Research in child psychology helps us understand why. Various studies have shown that toddlers who are raised in homes of love, stability, and warmth are the most likely to pursue new experiences and to take emotional risks. Because they know they have a competent and loving adult they can return to, they feel safe to explore.

But if we didn't grow up in such a home, we will often draw a line, build a fence, and decide to experience Jesus' love on the cross, but we won't risk trusting the love that sent him there.

In doing this, we are negating much of the reason Jesus became a man in the first place. Grasp the significance of these verses:

- "Because whatever the Father does the Son also does." (John@5:19)
- "Anyone who has seen me has seen the Father." (John@14:9)
- "Don't you believe that I am in the Father, and that the Father is in me?" (John@14:10)

- "Believe me when I say that I am in the Father and the Father is in me." (John@14:11)
- "When you pray, say: "[*Abba*], hallowed be your name." (Luke@11:2)

Jesus came to make God's love tangible to you and me. But for many of us, the tainted love of our earthly fathers has poisoned the love we experience from our Father in heaven.

To see if this has been the case for you, take this tainted-love litmus test. Read the following passage out of a psalm of David, and ask yourself, "What did David do that made God so angry?"

The earth trembled and quaked, and the foundations of the mountains shook; they trembled because he was angry. Smoke rose from his nostrils; consuming fire came from his mouth, burning coals blazed out of it. He made darkness his covering, his canopy around him . . . The LORD thundered from heaven; the voice of the Most High resounded. The valleys of the sea were exposed and the foundations of the earth laid bare at your rebuke, O LORD, at the blast of breath from your nostrils. (Psalm@18:7-8,11,13,15)

So much for the *Mr. Roger's Neighborhood* type of love we expect from God. David must have done something pretty ornery to get God that chapped. I can remember the panic in my heart when I made my dad mad as a kid. Especially the time my brother and I were behind a bush shooting bottle rockets at cars as they rounded the corner of our street. Unfortunately, my parents came home early from shopping. As they rounded that corner, they drove straight into a bottle rocket assault. Was my dad ticked! But his wrath was balanced and cool compared to God's wrath in this story.

So, what do you think David did? It sure is apparent that God was miffed. I mean, how angry would he have to be to make *darkness* his covering? Do you think he was ticked about David's little bathtub scandal with Bathsheba? Or his choice to kill her husband instead of come clean with his own lustful passions? Do you think that maybe God really was embarrassed with the whole naked dancing thing?

If you think any of those things, you are wrong. And you pass the tainted-love test, making it likely that you have a tainted view of God's love. God was indeed angry, but not at David. Let's look at the verse that started this whole wrath-of-God scenario:

> The cords of the grave coiled around me; the snares of death confronted me. In my distress I called to the LORD; I cried to my God for help. From his temple he heard my voice; my cry came before him, into his ears. The earth trembled and quaked, and the foundations of the mountains shook. (Psalm@18:5-7)

Do you see it? Do you see what really makes God mad? What really makes God angry is when the Enemy is picking on his kids! He hates the ravages of sin and the tactics of the devil's hordes. God the Father loves his kids! David got brutally honest with God and cried out to him for help. God heard that cry and came with the full force of his might to help him.

This same love sent the full force of God's mercy and forgiveness to the cross to conquer the enemy of our souls, once and for all. But God doesn't just love humanity that much, he loves *you* that much.

I meet people almost weekly whose fathers are terrible representations of what God intended dads to be. These fathers abandoned, abused, manipulated, neglected, and infected them—and gave their kids a tainted view of their Father in heaven.

But our earthly father's abuse in the past is no excuse for avoiding our heavenly Father's love in the present. If we want to escape suburbia, we must admit we have a tainted perspective of God's love, and we must ask him to lead us into the new territory of knowing. We must risk believing in a perfect Father's perfect love.

As we explore God's love, I believe he begins to restore a sense of wonder, awe, and childlike trust to our desolate spirituality.

Our relationship with our heavenly Father works much like a healthy relationship between a parent and child. Just as parents can nurture wonder in their kids by giving them opportunities to interact with their environment and ask questions that bring understanding, so does God.

When my inquisitive daughter was a toddler, I would often take her on walks, and she would ask me things like:

- "Daddy, where does the *white* go when snow melts?"
- "Daddy, do earth worms ever sneeze?"
- "Daddy, how does a whale poop?"
- "Daddy, how much does God weigh?"

It is a parent's job to nurture a sense of wonder in our kids. Not only does wonder develop intelligence as children grow, I believe it also helps kids maintain their sense of innocence.

Our heavenly Father longs to restore our own innocence and sense of wonder. He does so by inviting us to explore the world and step outside of our comfortable and cozy churches and experience the largest sanctuary of all, creation. The best way to experience a renewed sense of wonder is to ask for it, and then slow down and look for it.

I used to get so frustrated when hiking on a rainforest trail with my kids. The problem was my misdirected goal. It used to be my goal was to get to the destination so we could look at the waterfall and then turn around and get back to the car. My kids have taught me to change my goals. My goal now is not the destination, but the experience. My kids love to stop and pick up sticks, look at centipedes, and ask all kinds of crazy questions. The amazing thing is that, when I slow down to embrace such distractions, I enjoy the walk so much more.

So slow down. Find a place where you can lie on your back, stare into the night sky, and actually count stars. Yes, you may have to leave suburbia for an evening to do so. Yes, you may have to forgo an evening of television to experience creation, but it will be worth it. Wrestle on the floor with your kids and realize how much God enjoys being with you. Smell a flower, write a poem of love, or just close your eyes and imagine Jesus laughing. So many of us are just too serious with God. Maybe that's the way our earthly fathers were with us, but we don't have to let our earthly fathers determine our heavenly Father's identity—now do we?

Maybe you have never considered that you could relate to God on such an intimate level. Perhaps God's love for you has remained an elusive theological concept or, at best, a warm, fuzzy feeling based on a worship song.

Escaping suburbia requires walking in a restored sense of

innocence. It means relating with God from a place of safety and childlike trust. It means spending your days with a renewed sense of wonder instead of criticism regarding the creation around you. Our heavenly Father bids us, "Come!" Shall we take him at his Word and give it a try?

▸STOP, ▸LOOK, & LISTEN

1. Is *Abba* Father trapped in the box of your childhood experiences? List the character and personality qualities of your childhood father (good and bad). Examine each one and ask God how it influences your perception of him as your heavenly Father.

2. God isn't really masculine or feminine like we perceive humans. So try the same exercise using the qualities of your mother.

To fully live the adventure God offers us, we must pass through various levels of intimacy in our relationship with God. This last one is the most satisfying level . . . and perhaps the most challenging to risk.

The Lover of Your Soul

For many, life in the kingdom of God is billed as having a personal relationship with Christ. But honestly, how personal is it? In spiritual suburbia, personal has become synonymous with private—nobody knows I have a relationship with Christ and sometimes even I forget.

But Jesus invites us, not into a belief system, but into a relationship. When he says, "I am the way and the truth and the life" (John@14:6), I believe he is inviting us to enter into a passionate love relationship with him.

I believe he is telling us that it is possible to know him, and for him to know us like husbands and wives know each other. Cindy and I have been married for sixteen years, and I feel an indescribable sense of completeness when I am around her. We share a deep level of intimacy and trust. I have chosen to share the deepest things in my life with her, and her only. I get naked with her and her only (I'm sure you are relieved to know that).

Marriage was created in paradise, and God intended this union to be a reflection of the relationship he desires with us. Not sexual of course, but emotionally intimate. Not erotic of course, but passionate. A reflection of what is possible when we get to know God at the deepest level of our beings, just like when we get to know another human being.

God invites us into a relationship of such trust and closeness that we feel completely safe with him . . . willing to be "naked" in his presence, with nothing to hide . . . willing to bridge any barrier in order to find complete oneness with him. To experience this deep level of intimacy with God, we need to risk feeling a little undignified and unruly in the presence of the lover of our soul.

Were you taught to obey the rules and just wait your turn to get to God, even if your heart is telling you that you need a hug, and *you need it now?* If so, take the risk to dance, hug, and grab hold of God.

That's what David did. He didn't care how others viewed his passion for God—his eyes were on God alone. He wrote: "May those who hope in you not be disgraced because of me, O Lord, the LORD Almighty; may those who seek you not be put to shame because of me, O God of Israel . . . for zeal for your house consumes me, and the insults of those who insult you fall on me" (Psalm@69:6,9).

Sometimes pursuing God may mean dancing or lying prostrate before the lover of your soul. It may mean pulling your car over to the side of the road and pursuing the sunset with your spirit instead of just your eyes. It may even mean studying your Bible during your lunch break to get to know God a little more, instead of studying your co-worker in order to get to know him or her a little more.

Most of all, pursuing intimacy at the deepest level means being willing to let go of some preconceived protocol and embrace a little more zeal and recklessness. After all, don't the worshippers that Scripture highlights tend to bend the rules or risk looking a little goofy in the process? There was the woman who was willing to embarrass herself and spill perfume all over Jesus (Matthew@26:7). There was the bizarre example of worship and warfare at Jericho (Joshua@6:7), and the magi who risked so much in order to worship someone far greater than they realized (Matthew@2:9). Often the deciding factor for me is where my deepest affections lie—toward pleasing God or toward gaining approval from others. Step out . . . do a little dance . . . and make a little love toward God tonight.

Worship should declare the joyous celebration of God's presence in our lives, the awesomeness of his sovereignty over the whole universe, and the tangibleness of a transparent, unashamed, and intimate love—just like God wants expressed through marriage. The ways that I express my affections for my wife are quite diverse, but my love for her should be evident every day that I celebrate her love in my life.

We should view worship as a lifestyle as well as a part of church meetings. In both instances, it is choosing to give all honor and thankfulness back to God for his presence in our lives. Although some contemporary religious styles often interpret reverence to God as something quiet and somber, scriptural worship is quite diverse. Biblical worship connotes freedom, ranging from standing, raising hands, or dancing, to kneeling or lying prostrate; from quiet, reflective listening to loud, passionate praise.

Do you need to get out of your rut as a worshipper? Spiritual suburbia places so many limits on what worship is and what it is not, that we spend most of our attention making sure we are doing it right instead of on Jesus himself. I encourage you to step outside your norm a bit this week. If contemporary praise and worship and "jumpin' in the house of God" is your norm, try reading and praying through a hymn or two. You may have to borrow one from Grandma or the church down the street. If structure and protocol are the norm for your worship experiences, see what happens if you raise your hands in adoration of your king or kneel in reverence before you are asked. Then take your worship home with you and ask God to increase your passion and desire for him in the private places of your life.

▸STOP, ▸LOOK, & LISTEN

1. Has your personal relationship with Jesus turned private and matter-of-fact? Marriage experts often recommend going on a weekly date with your spouse to rekindle romance.... What would that look like for you and Jesus?

2. How have your current or past romantic relationships influenced your ability to draw near to God?

A Never-Ending Adventure

How far can this exploration of intimacy with God go? The potential is as endless as God is eternal. That's the beauty of plumbing the depths of the unfathomable. The adventure never ends.

There is a story I once heard of a young man who went to a wise spiritual leader and asked, "I want to know God like you do. Can you teach me?"

"To know God as I do you'll have to follow me," the leader said as he walked toward the sandy shore of the sea.

The teacher then had the young apprentice follow him out until they were chest deep in the water. Suddenly, he grabbed the boy and held his head under the water.

At first the boy thought, *This is strange, but I'll go along with it.* Then, as his oxygen supply began to thin, he struggled a bit, trying to communicate to the sage that it was time to come up—yet the sage held him firm. Struggle turned to panic and the apprentice kicked and thrashed and finally broke free.

"What the hell do you think you are doing?" he shouted at the wise man he once admired.

"When you want God as desperately as you wanted air, you will know him as I do," came the unruffled reply.

How far can this journey outside the boundaries of suburbia take us? Deep . . . desperately deep. Charles Finney wrote of experiencing God's love in such a way that he thought it would kill him.

Without any expectation of it, without ever having the thought in my mind that there was any such thing for me, without any recollection that I had ever heard the

thing mentioned by any person in the world, the Holy
Ghost descended on me in a manner that seemed to go
through me, body and soul.

I could feel the impression, like a wave of electricity,
going through and through me. Indeed it seemed to
come in waves and waves of liquid love. . . .

No words can express the wonderful love that was
shed abroad in my heart. I wept aloud with joy and
love. . . . The waves came over me, and over me, one
after the other, until I recollect I cried out, "I shall die if
these waves continue to pass over me." I said, "Lord, I
cannot bear any more;" yet I had no fear of death.[1]

How incredible to experience God's presence as liquid
waves of love! Ah, but we have become content living with so
little of God's presence. Life in spiritual suburbia seems to have
convinced us that there are more important things to pursue
than a deep, meaningful, and rich relationship with our Maker.
Yet that is what we are created for. God designed us to long to
pursue him. We are relational people. We love a relational God.

Perhaps that is why the Enemy works so hard to counterfeit
healthy relationships and places so many distractions around
us. The Devil does not want you going deeper, growing further,
or experiencing more in your relationship with God. If you did,
your love for God might become contagious. Others might
become more thirsty and hungry for substance in their own
relationships with God. Next thing you know, there could actually be revival happening in our lives, our homes, our churches,
and our cities.

So the Devil and life work hard to keep you and me so busy
that our relationship with God can only be maintained at some

mediocre level. Just enough so we don't feel like we are failing. The problem is, many of us are stirring. Many of us are tired of living in a superficial relationship with God when we sense there is so much more. Suburbia has lost its appeal. Our souls are hungry for more of the real presence of God. We don't just want him to deliver the pizza to us, we want him to come inside our souls and share the meal with us.

▸STOP, ▸LOOK, & LISTEN

1. Though some segments of the church are good at pretending, we can not manufacture authentic experiences, such as the one Finney had. Just get honest with God for a moment. Would you like to experience his love at that depth? If so, at what price or sacrifice?

2. Numerous people of the Christian faith report such experiences. Read about the spiritual disciplines that aided in that journey. For starters read *The Practice of the Presence of God* by Brother Lawrence or *Deeper Experiences of Famous Christians* by James Gilchrist Lawson.

CHAPTER SEVEN

A PERFECT
LAWN

On Brokenness

I KNOCKED ON CHARLIE and Susan's door half hoping they wouldn't answer. I still wasn't sure I wanted to go through the superficial holiday greetings and obligatory "How are yous." But I needed to borrow some sugar, and I didn't want to make the effort to drive to the store.

I've got to try something different this time. Maybe a "wow" your Christmas lights look great! Can I have some sugar?

Susan opened the door and I blurted out, "Hey Susan. It's me, Eric, from next door. How are you? Can I borrow some sugar?"

Dang . . . Old habits die hard.

Susan looked a little more sheepish than I remembered from our last interaction some six months prior. But maybe that's because it is now the rainy Northwest winter season, and that was summer.

"Uh, sure," she said. "I saw you coming up the steps and thought maybe you were here to see Charlie. Come in."

Thinking quickly with my nimble social skills I responded, "Yep, sugar and to see Charlie. How is he doing?"

"It looks like he only has a couple weeks left to live," she continued. "The cancer is really taking its toll on his body and emotions. I figured since you are a priest, or whatever you said you were, that you might be coming over to comfort him."

Geez . . . I had no idea this was going on right next door. More nimble social skills or not? Not, I decided.

"Honestly, Susan, I had no idea," I confessed. "I'm so sorry. Is there anything I can do right now to help?"

"If you would be so kind as to go downstairs and visit with him that would be nice," came her compassionate and forgiving response. "I'll get your sugar."

Great. I've never even been in this house, and these guys have been my neighbors for two years now. What do I do? Where are the stairs?

I headed toward the hallway, figuring that was the most logical way to find the steps downstairs. Susan gently caught my attention and pointed me to the doorway in the other direction.

As I descended, my senses were overwhelmed with the stuff cancer is made of. The air was moist, the smell was sterile and . . . and . . . if you've ever been around the dying, you know that smell. Indescribably unique, it is.

But the contrast visually was stunning. On the walls surrounding my descent and into the main room were posters of every size, made of the brightest colors and images. Computer-drawn images of seashores and sunsets, exotic animals and wild women, classic cars and modern aircraft. It was a veritable potpourri of computer art.

Charlie was the artist. Charlie, my neighbor, the man dying of cancer, whose basement door I had never seen, was an incredible artist.

"I want to die down here with my creations," he said. "I

dream of going to a better place when this is over. Maybe like that one over there," and pointed to an image of a isolated island with a lone palm tree and a well-endowed beach beauty.

"Do you think there is something after we go, Eric?"

We talked for quite awhile, Charlie and I. We talked of life. We talked about our dreams. We talked about how we are the luckiest men in the world to have the wives we have, despite our pasts. We talked of the God I believe in and the One he didn't.

Charlie and I had a number of visits, but they turned out to be way too few. Then, one day, he was gone.

When I looked at Charlie's house on the outside, I would never have guessed the decay going on inside. Everything on the outside appeared so smooth, so together, so whole.

Walk down the sidewalks of most suburbs, and you'll see perfectly manicured lawns, trimmed bushes, and oil-free driveways. Most of us would rather ignore real-world broken-ness — sickness, poverty, busted relationships, and past abuses, just to name a few. So we focus on keeping our own lawns green and our bushes trimmed. We like the manicured look and hate the idea of a brown, patchy lawn. Water it. Fertilize it. Patch up the bald spots. That's what we prefer. That's why we hide our hurting lives and try so hard to keep up appearances.

But we're talking about the real lives of people, not the manu-factured story of some lawn gnome. We're talking about people like you and me, walking in their own brand of brokenness.

Just Beneath the Surface

Emily was thirsty. This was day two of her mommy's boyfriend's unwillingness to move from the couch to help her while he maintained his methamphetamine buzz. She tried to get his attention, but to him Emily was only a distraction on his perpetual journey to nirvana. Mommy hadn't been home since she left on "business" and had cast off this precious three-year-old to his care. Regardless of circumstances, her dirty face and matted blonde hair couldn't hide the childlike innocence that sparkled in her blue eyes. She would continue to fend for herself, for this was her world.

Emily assumed that all little girls live this way. This was the normal routine for her. She pried open the refrigerator looking for something to drink. The milk, as she discovered yesterday, was curdled and tasted yucky. The apple juice was long since gone. She couldn't open a beer bottle without help, but thought she could reach the jar of clear liquid tucked back in the corner.

She stretched and grabbed the lidless Mason jar with her tiny hands. As she lifted it and began to pour it into her mouth, she suddenly felt a burning sensation beginning to consume her. The hydrochloric acid that her mommy and boyfriend used to make their drug of choice was beginning to eat away at her flesh like the meth it produced had been eating away at her childhood.

The screams roused the boyfriend, who had just enough sense to take her to the hospital. In his warped mind he knew bringing an ambulance to the house would have meant surefire arrest for drug possession. By the time they reached the hospital, Emily's screams had died to just a whimper. The acid had burned a hole in her mouth and scorched her esophagus. Thankfully, none had been ingested, but the melted flesh on her chin and chest told the doctors that this little girl teetered on life. They had only minutes left to save her, and thankfully, they did.

Emily is better now, and living with a family that values her more than manufactured highs. Hers is the picture I see whenever I ponder the outcome of walking in the brokenness of addiction.

But stories of brokenness abound.

Not long ago, a young woman came to me wanting to know if I would perform her wedding ceremony. She had been living with a guy for over a year and was eager to be his wife. Over the course of our conversation, she explained how he periodically slips up with other women, regularly masturbates to porn, and hits her when he is angry.

"But he means well and is a really nice guy," came her defense when I challenged the sanity of such an arrangement. "Besides, if I marry him, I won't have to be alone again, and maybe he will stay more faithful."

This child of God walks in the brokenness of loneliness. She would rather have an abusive relationship with a man than no relationship at all.

Then there is my friend and a former pastor, whom I'll call Steve. Five years into the ministry, and he regularly found himself starting his day with Oswald Chamber's *My Utmost for His Highest*, but finishing it with an hour of Satan's eye-candy, furnished by some porn website. Steve lived in his own private hell, fearing that if he shared the truth with his congregation, they would crucify him. Finally, he did share, and they indeed did crucify him. . . . Steve lives in the world of spiritual knowledge, but walks the sidewalks of sexual brokenness.

Brokenness and pain are not pretty. They are like a throbbing sore, constantly aching and oozing until we medicate or anesthetize them. Life in suburbia encourages us to hide the ugly or uncomfortable or painful parts of our lives from others and from God. After all, no one else seems broken.

But brokenness lurks inside all of us. As we grow older, we may forget about the causes of that pain, but we still live with its consequences. Like a sinkhole covered up by a veneer of green grass, brokenness causes God's presence and power to fade like an echo in our soul. The good news is it doesn't have to be that way! The truth is, the area of our deepest pain often has the potential to be the source of our greatest joy and the launching pad of our highest callings.

Think about the addict who has been clean for one year. What joy he discovers in God's ability to clean him up. After ten years of living clean that same addict is often even more thankful for God's redemptive work and often spends time helping others find freedom as well. Indeed, those who have been forgiven much tend to love much.

Broken Jars and Whole Lives

Suburbia gives us shame in our brokenness; Jesus gives us hope. The church often says, "How could you?" The Holy Spirit says, "I still love you." Our culture finds no value in broken things; God finds redemptive value in them.

Case in point: remember the story of the woman who broke the jar of perfume and poured it on Jesus' head? The gospel of Mark puts it this way:

> While he was in Bethany, reclining at the table in the home of a man known as Simon the Leper, a woman came with an alabaster jar of very expensive perfume, made of pure nard. She broke the jar and poured the perfume on his head. Some of those present were

saying indignantly to one another, "Why this waste of perfume? It could have been sold for more than a year's wages and the money given to the poor." And they rebuked her harshly. "Leave her alone," said Jesus. "Why are you bothering her? She has done a beautiful thing to me."(Mark@14:3-6)

Almost everyone who witnessed this display of extravagant worship placed value on the jar of perfume before it was broken. But Jesus placed value on it after it was broken. This woman was broken before him, and he was pleased.

What would have happened if she had listened to the voices of those around her?

Whose voice are you listening to regarding your brokenness?

This is a story of worship that God likes. The same story he wants us to live today. He is drawn to people who admit and invite him into their brokenness. I am convinced that is why the Father had Jesus be born in a manger. He wanted his Son to be born in the brokenness of poverty. God didn't choose for Jesus to be born into the seeming togetherness of the elite or the rich. His Son was born in one of the lowest cities of the day, but even that must not have been low enough, for Jesus was born in a stable that housed only animals.

Most of us understand theologically that God humbled himself and became a human being. And many of us profess to believe that God chose a stable to show us that there is no place on earth he will not go to reach us with his love.

But what if it was more than that?

What if God the Father was trying to tell us his life can best be born out in the lowest, most shameful places of humanity? What if he was not only talking about the physical stuff of earth, but the hidden stuff in our souls as well? Could those dark, shameful, broken places that we work so hard to hide actually be the places God's life has the best chance of shining forth from?

When Jesus was born, a light in the night sky pointed to the place in Bethlehem where seekers could come and tangibly experience God's love. Is that same light now shining on the dark parts of our souls so that others can see God's redemptive work in our lives? Could my brokenness, which the Enemy intended to be a curse, actually be used as a gift?

The parts of our lives that we have tried so desperately to hide or patch over are the very places that God wants to bring his redemptive power and life! After Jesus' birth, lowly Bethlehem became a sacred and holy site. When God's life came and invaded darkness, the world got the blessing and the Father got the glory. The same can happen in our lives, if we allow God's life to be born anew in our hurts and pains.

Does this amaze you as much as it amazes me? I've often thought that God's goodness is best reflected in the polished parts of my life. Cuz that's the way it is in suburbia. When I drive down the street, I notice my neighbor's freshly waxed BMW or the newly painted picket fence. I don't look in their garbage or slither through the crawl space under their houses. Leave it to God to set my world backward. He wants to bring light to my darkness, to recycle my garbage, and clean out my crawl spaces. He shows up, not to admire my wax job, but to heal my rust spots. Even the most profane places of my heart become life-giving and sacred when God is in the midst of them. In God's economy, broken things actually can have great value.

This book does not have room to communicate the pleth-ora of ways God uses to bring us life and healing. And honestly, that is not my point. I want to encourage you to trust and seek Jesus as he leads you through the land of brokenness to a place of wholeness.

Those of us who are living in spiritual suburbia are focusing on keeping our lawn looking perfect, while inside we are broken and hurt. We work so hard to prop up the exterior of our decent Christian living that we fail to attend to the hurts, hang-ups, and decay within. If we long to escape spiritual suburbia, we can no longer hide our brokenness. We must offer it to God as uncharted territory and be willing to explore it with him, beginning with surrender.

▸STOP, ▸LOOK, & LISTEN

1. What is the darkest place in your soul? What thing have you done (or had done to you) that few people, if any, know about? Revisit that wounding experience. Have you learned to numb it, ignore it, or just live with it? Are you willing to let God's love for you heal it?

2. Often brokenness is masked by addiction and addiction is masked by secrets. Are you hiding certain behaviors for fear of being caught or ashamed? If so, what is your behavior anesthetizing?

Surrender Versus Commitment

Many who struggle with the continuous ache of brokenness first try all kinds of things to anesthetize it: drugs, alcohol, shopping, and cyclic relationships. We may try yoga, yogurt, or Yoda . . . popularity, power, or porn . . . dressing up, dressing down, or complete nakedness. The list of ways we anesthetize ourselves is endless. But sooner or later, we find that those things only serve to widen the chasm created by brokenness. So we make a promise. . . .

You know what I mean. How often do we proclaim something like this to ourselves, or to our loved ones:

- "That's it. I'm never doing that again."
- "I've had enough, that's the last time I . . ."
- "I promise, I'll never look . . . touch . . . go there . . . take that . . . eat that . . . lust after that again."

Most people can go for ninety days maximum with such Superman willpower. But then we stumble again. Sin, repent, commit to change . . . sin, repent, commit to change . . . round and round the cycle goes. When we will crash and burn, nobody knows.

But herein lies the problem—commitment. As long as we are committed to overcoming our brokenness, we won't be able to do so. I'm sorry, but you and I just don't have the mental or physical fortitude to overcome our own brokenness. What we really need to do is surrender.

Paul understood the war that raged within him when he said:

I have the desire to do what is good, but I cannot carry it out. For what I do is not the good I want to do; no, the evil I do not want to do—this I keep on doing . . . What a wretched man I am! Who will rescue me from this body of death? Thanks be to God—through Jesus Christ our Lord! (Romans@7:18-19,24-25)

Brother Paul struggled like we do. We try so hard and then so often fail. How many times has despair washed over my faith because a moment of indulgence crushed a month of success? Maybe it's time to admit that if I keep doing what I've always done (try harder), I'll keep getting what I've always gotten (failure at some point). Maybe it's time to surrender to a source greater than myself.

The biggest difference between commitment and surrender is who you put in control: God or yourself. Give up trying to overcome your hurt, addiction, and brokenness. Surrender. It is the only way you will succeed.

I know it sounds a bit freakish, but surrender may not be what you think it is.

Surrender is not losing the battle. Many of us fear we only have two choices: either fight harder to overcome our brokenness, or give in to it and let it crush our lives to pieces under its weight. The truth is that it is possible to surrender the battle to God and let him fight for you.

Surrender is not periodically giving in to your hurt and/or brokenness. To surrender doesn't mean to binge and purge on your pain. It means admitting that what you have always done isn't working and that you need to find a new way that will lead to wholeness and freedom.

Surrender is not something only weak or cowardly people do. In fact, surrendering is one of the bravest things you can do, because it is trusting your life to something or someone else. This is a very vulnerable place to walk.

Surrender is not giving up a part of your life. When soldiers surrender in a battle, they give up their entire beings into the hands of the one they surrender to. When you came to Christ, you surrendered it all to him anyway. He knew what he was getting; the question is did you know what you were giving?

When Jesus begins to explore the land of our brokenness with us, he wants to know we have surrendered it all. Look at the desolate territory of your soul and ask him, "Can you redeem this land?" If he says yes, then surrender it to him. Give up trying to fix it to impress him or trying to hide it to protect him.

One of the hardest areas for me to surrender was my idea that I needed to have it together in front of those I pastor or lead. I can't recall exactly when I bought into the lie, but I'm sure the Enemy gave it to me with a teaspoon of sugar. I have spent a lot of years feeling responsible for other people's walk with God. You know, the whole "live above reproach" thing. The problem arises when living above reproach becomes synonymous with hiding behind dishonesty.

When I was a child in the faith, I wanted to be a preacher when I grew up. I longed to preach purposefully, like Greg Laurie of the Harvest Crusades, or powerfully, like John Wimber of the Vineyard Movement, or with professional presence, like Chuck Swindoll of Insight for Living. Each of them, *in my mind's eye*, had it sooo together. I imagined them walking around with a bright, shiny halo, like the saints on the walls of great cathedrals.

My imagination was filling in the gaps of their daily existence with what I saw and heard on stage. When I compared their lives to mine, I saw how I still struggled day-to-day. It was then I realized there wasn't much hope for me—unless, of course, I pretended . . .

During that early season of my walk, God gave me an opportunity to have lunch with a prominent pastor and hero of mine, Tom Stipe. During our chat, Tom must have picked up on my naïve, man of God "idol worship." Gently, but firmly, he said, "Eric, there are no Cinderella stories in the kingdom of God. Every authentic leader you've said you admire bears the scars of brokenness. If they don't walk with a limp, they probably aren't worthy to be followed."

Walking with a limp is not only an indication of struggle and past brokenness, but also evidence of healing and perseverance. God meets us in our places of brokenness and pain and gives us the ability to move on. Right then, over a cheeseburger and fries, God gave me an opportunity to learn via the wisdom of another. He wanted me to understand that maturity in faith and consistent living is more than a stage show. Unfortunately, Tom's words were drowned out by my own preconceived ideas.

The Bible tells us that God's gift and his call are irrevocable (Romans@11:29), but so is the path to get there. God doesn't intend for us to take short cuts on the way to holiness and healing. He was asking me to surrender my need to perform and pretend in order to impress others. One way or another, I was going to have to learn to surrender.

When we short-circuit the process and don't allow ourselves to be broken at the foot of the cross, we will find ourselves building our own kingdom and not God's. Now, years later, I find myself telling those whom I mentor the same thing Tom told me. Oh, I hope they listen better than I did. Because surrender requires honesty, not duplicity.

▸STOP, ▸LOOK, & LISTEN

1. How many things have you "committed" to fix in yourself? (Weight, porn, gossip, a critical spirit, fear, drugs, and so on.) What would surrender look like in that area?

2. Surrender your pride this week and share an area of brokenness with someone you can trust. If you need to, just blame your reason for sharing on this book. I'll take the heat for you.

Honesty Versus Duplicity

Spiritual suburbia is full of posers. The problem with being a poser is that your movements are restricted. Posers can't explore uncharted areas, but instead are forced to keep up the appearance of their glittering images. In spiritual suburbia, every life needs to look the same so that no difference can be felt or recognized. We learn to pose for each other, pretending to be what we perceive others want us to be, while our souls begin to wither and scream for relief. Our insides decay while our outsides obey.

"How are you today?" is the standard question with no anticipated answer.

"Fine," comes our standard answer, no intended meaning. The truth is we are FINE (Freaked out, Insecure, Neurotic, and Emotional).

God will only be able to bring his redemptive power if we are honest and admit we need his help. When it comes to honesty, we have to walk the way of the cross. We must give up our rights, privileges, and personal expectations, trusting God's divine guidance and purpose instead. We must be brutally honest with God and ourselves, and then brutally honest with others. Vertical honesty, and then horizontal honesty. Being honest and living in duplicity are not compatible lifestyles.

As I look around the American evangelical church, I see a sort of Wonderbra spirituality. We use whatever contraption we can to puff up what little substance we actually have to impress others, even if it hurts us in the process. Then, sooner or later, when we find ourselves entering into an intimate relationship with another, they find out we really weren't as attractive as we made ourselves out to be. Perhaps the ultimate irony is that by enhancing our weaknesses, we may be distracting others from our strengths. Honesty allows us to say, "This is who I am, and I need you to love me despite what it looks like."

Do we honestly think that when we Wonderbra God, we are fooling him? He knows us as we really are, puffed up or pooched out, and what we need to experience his total acceptance and love.

The psalmist wrote,

Give thanks to the LORD, for he is good.
His love endures forever.
Give thanks to the God of gods.
His love endures forever.
who by his understanding made the heavens,
His love endures forever.
to him who divided the Red Sea asunder
His love endures forever.
to him who led his people through the desert,
His love endures forever.
Give thanks to the God of heaven.
His love endures forever.
(Psalm@136:1-2,5,13,16,26)

Is it just me, or do you see a pattern in this passage? In twenty-six verses, David retells the story of God's power and intervention in the world and in the lives of his people. Twenty-six times in twenty-six verses, David connects God's story with God's love. In monumental times and in mundane times, God's love is the common denominator in history and in David's life. If anything should cause our backs to stand a little straighter, our shoulders to be a little broader, and our chests to expand a little further, it is the reality that *God's love endures*—even throughout my story.

His love for me didn't decrease one iota during my years of brokenness. Nor has it increased during my years of growth either. It has remained pure, lavish, purposeful, and powerful over all these years. At least something is consistent in my life. . . .

Vertical honesty doesn't only mean that I am transparent with God about who I am, but it also means that I'm receptive *to who he is in all his love.* False messages and mistakes may tell me that I don't deserve God's love, and perhaps this is true. But just because I don't deserve it, doesn't mean that I can't have it. It is his gift to give and only my choice to receive.

But it's not enough to simply be vertically honest. Escaping suburbia and being healed of our brokenness also requires horizontal honesty. To help you understand why, let's return to our discussion of Wonderbra spirituality. When we Wonderbra the church, we are only reinforcing duplicity. The body of Christ is already propped up and restricted enough. I propose that some of us need to just bare it all (our souls) and be free.

If you have ever participated in any type of healthy recovery group, Alcoholics Anonymous, Narcotics Anonymous, Celebrate Recovery, U-Turn for Christ, and so on, you've seen the power of honesty firsthand. Coming clean with a bunch of addicts is amazingly freeing in these contexts. But when people come clean in the church, the response is often quite different.

Take, for instance, the time my friend Amy talked about her eating disorder and struggle with food with my church Bible study group. After the initial under-our-breath gasps of, "We had no idea," the group piled on her like a school of well-meaning piranhas. Everyone wanted a piece of "helping" Amy find the way to healing. After about a half-hour of counsel and storytelling from the group, Amy sheepishly piped up again, "I was just asking for prayer."

The church needs to follow the recovery group model. These days, I have a small group Bible study that includes numerous methamphetamine addicts who participate regularly in Narcotics Anonymous (NA). Yes, I realize they think they are joining us to work on their own journey to freedom, but I have learned something just as valuable from them. When someone else shares pain or shame within the group, my recovery friends have an incredible response. This recovery group seems to provide a greater catalyst toward wholeness than twenty minutes of my wisdom or ten minutes of someone's storytelling.

When someone shares his or her struggle, the addicts in the group simply respond, "Thank you for sharing." No judgment, no critique, no shaming. Just genuine thankfulness that someone was . . . well . . . honest. Now no one has to pretend anymore, which is the first step toward healing. Whether we pray for them, counsel them, or move on is up to them. It is their journey; we are just there to help.

Of course, sharing like this in a group of committed posers can make a person feel as welcome as a transvestite ballerina in a punk mosh pit. So be careful where you choose to dance. Still, I have found that most people are really tired of pretending to be something they are not. When one person decides to take off his or her happy mask and put it on the shelf, others will follow.

The place where honesty on the horizontal and vertical meet looks remarkably like a cross. Something I learned from the "Red Pill Forum."

Walking Toward Versus Walking Away

Not long ago, I had the privilege of facilitating a group of twelve spiritually hungry and brutally honest seekers. Their backgrounds were as diverse as their biblical perceptions. One person was a self-styled Buddhist, another was raised and burned in the Christian church, and still another held strongly to a sort of Northwest, New Age, environmentalist spirituality. We had a hypno-therapist, a massage therapist, a sex therapist, and even a black belt karate champion. We had a worship leader, wilderness survival guide, and a short, bald, somewhat insecure pastor (me) in our midst.

How this group of dissimilar pilgrims came together is a story for another book. But the beauty is that we came together with two simple rules and one goal: (1) A commitment to honesty about our own life and (2) a commitment to honor the honesty in each other's lives. Our goal was exploring God's story in Christianity, without manipulation or pressure to convert. The members of the group sincerely wanted to explore faith and the mystery of Jesus without all the infomercial Christianity commonly associated with it. In other words they wanted to take an honest look at the vertical of their lives within the context of safe, horizontal relationships. The place where those worlds crossed was the landscape in which they asked me to guide the discussion.

I affectionately dubbed our ragamuffin group the "Red Pill Forum," alluding to the first *Matrix* movie, and the scene where Neo had to choose either the red pill or the blue pill. Choosing the red pill meant discovering the truth and following it despite not really knowing just how far that journey would go. Choosing the blue pill meant erasing the question and going back to pretending everything was fine . . . FINE. This group's version of choosing the "red pill" was swallowing a weekly reading from Brian McClaren's challenging but non-condescending book *Finding Faith*.

I had no idea how hard it would be for me to allow others to be honest about how they felt about something that I valued so dearly. Could I allow someone to tell the group how they felt about a God who would allow someone as spiritual as Confucius to go to hell and yet save someone as horrid as serial killer Ted Bundy? I badly wanted to "fix" every theological quandary, but instead I spent most of my time focusing on the challenge to simultaneously bite my tongue and yet be able to say, "Thank you for being honest."

Somehow, I knew the Holy Spirit was asking me to trust the process, to be a guide to truth and not truth itself. I needed to let a bridge of love be built so that the group could bear the weight of confrontation. Little did I know that the biggest burden would not be from a weight I had placed on the group, but by a weight they would place on me.

It happened about the seventh week of our weekly gatherings. I was talking about how Jesus invites us to live from a whole new perspective—a perspective in which life is lived from a "God-ward" orientation and not a "self-ward" orientation. My now much-esteemed karate friend unloaded a simple statement that besmirched my neat and tidy Christian suburbia like graffiti on a wedding cake.

She said, "That's one thing I don't understand. Christians talk so much about the abundant life, but it seems all your decisions are based on fear. It seems you Christians come to Christ because you are afraid of going to hell. . . . You live a 'good' life so that God won't punish you or the church won't get mad at you. . . . You don't share your faults because you are afraid of looking bad . . . fear, fear, fear. Fear of hell, fear of punishment, fear of displeasing God or others—honestly, that doesn't sound like abundance to me."

Ouch, that really hurt. She risked honesty because she felt safe enough to be honest. I received her honesty because I felt safe enough not to be defensive. Our dialogue launched me on a week of thinking about decisions that I had made in my faith journey.

How often do I make a decision because I am walking away from something instead of walking toward something?

I was amazed to realize that so many of my decisions are based on avoiding pain rather than on pursuing goodness. On trying not to mess up again instead of moving toward the wholeness Jesus offers. I was stunned to see how many of my decisions were aimed at not disappointing God, my family, or my church, instead of honoring God, my family, or my church. That's not abundance, that's avoidance!

No wonder so many of us remain stuck in spiritual suburbia! We need a shift in perspective. God doesn't invite us out of suburbia and into the land of brokenness so that we can become fixated on what is wrong in our lives. He invites us into that dark, unexplored place so that we can see his re-creative power at work. He doesn't want us focused on avoiding pain. He wants us focused on pursuing wholeness.

As you open the gate and step outside the protective fence you may have placed around those shadowy areas of your life—pursue peace, pursue healing, pursue Christ. We spend so much time attending to the exterior of our lives; maybe it is time to invest some time, energy, and money on the inside. After all, that is where we really live. Behind the doorway, life happens. Friendships can grow, love can heal, and passion can deepen. Our choice is whether it continues to decay, due to neglect, or to become whole and functional again, due to care and attention. I know which one I choose. . . . Do you?

▸STOP, ▸LOOK, & LISTEN

1. Take stock of the decisions you make today. How many of them are made to avoid something? Pay special attention to moral decisions that involve interactions with other people.

2. What is the next step you need to take toward wholeness? Is it surrender, honesty, or pursuit? What things are keeping you from moving toward God's best for you?

CONCLUSION

RETHINKING
SUBURBIA

AWHILE BACK, I WAS having a late night latte, which helps my late nights go even later, with Brad, a thirty-something pastor friend of mine. We were sharing church-life experiences, yakking about the challenges of being young pastors, delving into the murky waters of theology so as to help each other feel smarter, and lamenting that most seminaries do a better job of teaching eschatology than they do teaching brokenology.

Okay, so I just made up a word. But Brad and I both knew that God wants to love the broken and hurting through the church. My problem was that I had too many messed-up people, and didn't know what to do to help them. Brad's problem was that he had too few messed-up people, and didn't know how to reach them.

His church started in the suburbs of a major California community. He said he had great people, great resources, great vision—but the church seemed unconnected to the rabble of culture that Jesus seemed to attract so easily. Then Brad made a statement that bore through my spiritual core like an angry mole on cocaine.

"Eric, the problem with suburbia is that it's perfectly designed to anesthetize us from pain. It puts a veneer of wholeness on the outside, and allows hollowness to thrive on the inside."

Ouch . . . that was sure sounding like my spiritual life.

By the end of another double shot of espresso, we decided there is no barrier that the power of God can't overcome when we give him permission—regardless of whether those barriers are from within or from without.

Since that conversation, my spiritual life has ebbed and flowed in and out of the suburbs. Some days my relationship with God seems as tangible and meaningful as a conversation over a cup of coffee with a good friend. Other times it lulls me into wanting to settle for a plastic Jesus who serves as a surrogate to the faith I really want to live. But I have found that there is, indeed, adventure in the purposeful releasing of God's presence in my life. Because this adventure requires that I leave the protection of predictability, I try to keep a couple of things in mind. I share them with you in hopes that they will help you drive off the pavement and into the abundant life and adventure that Jesus offers.

1. Have a clear vision of what you really want out of your relationship with God.

When I was a university professor, students would often come into my office asking for help planning their courses. They always came just before the next term's registration was to begin. Some would ask for insight into which professor they would be most compatible with (which was the easiest), some for help in deciding between two required courses that were in conflict during the school day. Others had no idea what they should take or why they were even at the university. We had a name for them—the perpetual undeclared major.

I didn't mind such indecision in freshmen and sophomores, because they were still exploring and finding the right path in life. But juniors and seniors who were still trying to figure out what they wanted to learn and do with their lives worried me. They were like ships without rudders, just drifting wherever the current took them.

Students with declared majors seldom had many choices between classes. Their course was mapped out for them on a timetable from their sophomore year until they graduated. When they graduated, they not only had a degree on a piece of paper, they had a substance to their education.

I remember talking with one student who thought that if he just took enough classes, sooner or later he would qualify for a degree in something and then he would graduate, almost as if by accident. He said he liked my sexuality course a lot; he enjoyed various art classes and had taken a number of the fisheries courses. I told him if he wasn't careful, he'd end up with a job drawing pictures of fish having sex, and that was a very narrow career field.

Haven't you found that life works better when you have vision and purpose? The truth is that if you have a clear vision of where you are going, you'll seldom be disappointed with where you've been. So, purpose not to get stuck in the monotony of spiritual suburbia. Don't allow yourself to be content with a McDonald's happy meal spiritual prize. Instead, purpose to experience the love and relationship that God has for you, even if the adventure takes you into the uncharted territory of your brokenness.

2. Give yourself permission to not be perfect.

Sometimes I find myself trying so hard to be something I'm not that I begin to not be something I am. What I am is God's beloved. What if, every day, I just accepted the fact that I'm not going to be perfect in anything I'm trying to accomplish in God's purpose and plan? Some might use this as an excuse to be sloppy with their faith, but that's not how I see it. From where I'm sitting, God's love deserves my best effort. I don't have to earn his love today—I just have to live in it and through it.

I'm not advocating that we serve God apathetically or without reverence. But we do need to be earnest and flexible. Like when my daughter plays soccer. She can play her best, and I can expect her to represent her family name in a good way on the field, but I don't have to expect her to be the next Mia Hamm. My daughter can even fail, and I'll still love her. She's still my daughter! So spend your day in the awareness that you are God's beloved. Living in this reality will release in you new freedom to fail, but fail in a forward direction.

The adventure awaits.

I long to sense mystery, depth, adventure, and hope in my relationship with God. I'm bored with predictability and hollowness. A long time ago, Jesus invited me to follow him as the Master of Life as he explores the dusty roads of my life and the dark alleys of the world around me. This time, I'm really going to surrender my artificial comfort and hang onto Jesus' divine intentions. Do you want to come with us? He always has room for more apprentices. . . .

To eternity and beyond,

Eric

NOTES

Chapter One: When Suburbia Loses Its Appeal

1. David Brooks, *On Paradise Drive* (New York: Simon & Schuster, 2004), 110.

Chapter Two: Keeping Up with the Joneses

1. Retrieved from http://www.wordspy.com/words/ metrosexual.asp.
2. Retrieved from http://www.brainydictionary.com/words/ pr/prodigal206993.html.
3. A. F. Kirkpatrick, *The Book of Psalms* (Grand Rapids, Mich.: Baker, 1982), 127.

Chapter Three: A Promising Career

1. Eugene Peterson, *The Message* (Intro to Galatians).
2. Retrieved from http://www.mertonfoundation.org/merton .php3?page=prayer.ext.

Chapter Four: A Television in Every Room

1. *Television and Health.* Retrieved December 9, 2005, from The Sourcebook for Teaching Science. http://www.csun .edu/~vceed002/health/docs/tv&health.html.
2. Richard N. Ostling, AP "Mother Teresa's Private Fears Told," *Peninsula Daily News.* Friday, October 17, 2003, C6.
3. Ostling, C6.
4. Ostling, C6.

5. Richard Foster, *Celebration of Discipline* (San Francisco: HarperSanFrancisco, 1978), 7.

Chapter Five: A Powerful SUV

1. James G. Lawson, *Deeper Experiences of Famous Christians* (Uhrichsville, Ohio: Barbour Publishing, Inc., 2000), 84.
2. Madame Guyon, "Praying the Scripture," *Devotional Classics: Selected Readings for Individuals and Groups*, eds. Richard Foster and James Bryan Smith (San Francisco: HarperSanFrancisco, 1993), 320-321.
3. Foster and Smith, eds., 320-321.
4. Julian of Norwich, "The Highest Form of Prayer," *Devotional Classics: Selected Readings for Individuals and Groups*, eds. Richard Foster and James Bryan Smith (San Francisco: HarperSanFrancisco, 1993), 71.
5. Brother Lawrence, *The Practice of the Presence of God*, second letter (Grand Rapids, Mich.: Revell, 1967), 36-37.

Chapter Six: A Really Big House

1. James G. Lawson, *Deeper Experiences of Famous Christians* (Uhrichsville, Ohio: Barbour, 2000), 209-210.

AUTHOR

ERIC SANDRAS is part of the next generation of leaders whom God is using to "raise the bar" in the relationships, faith, and life decisions of today's traditional and emergent churches. He is passionate about family, faith issues, and having extra butter on his popcorn at the movie theater. Eric and Cindy, his wife of sixteen years, have two wonderful children, Dakota Jasmine and Carter William. Prior to entering the pastorate, Eric spent almost ten years as a professor of Human Sexuality and Human Development at various Northwest universities and colleges. Eric and his family have recently relocated to Lancaster, California, where he is now the teaching pastor for the Desert Vineyard Christian Fellowship.

MAYBE IT'S TIME YOUR FAITH GOT NAKED.

Buck-Naked Faith

Eric Sandras, PhD
1-57683-525-1

How has your faith weathered postmodern pressures? Is it more pomp and circumstance than action and substance?

See your faith for what it is—when it's buck-naked and free of pretense. Only then can you decide if your days of stunted, make-believe faith are over. Find out how satisfying life can be as you refuse to accept anything less than an honest, cooperative friendship with God.

Honest and gritty, Eric Sandras wants to encourage a generation of believers to drop the layers of make-believe that stunt our spiritual growth. He exposes the naked truth: We need to dress our lives with a real friendship with God and nothing else.

Visit your local Christian bookstore, call NavPress at 1-800-366-7788,
or log on to www.navpress.com to purchase.
To locate a Christian bookstore near you, call 1-800-991-7747.

NAVPRESS
BRINGING TRUTH TO LIFE
www.navpress.com